Quirky Mandalas

Coloring Book for Adults

by Christea Blue

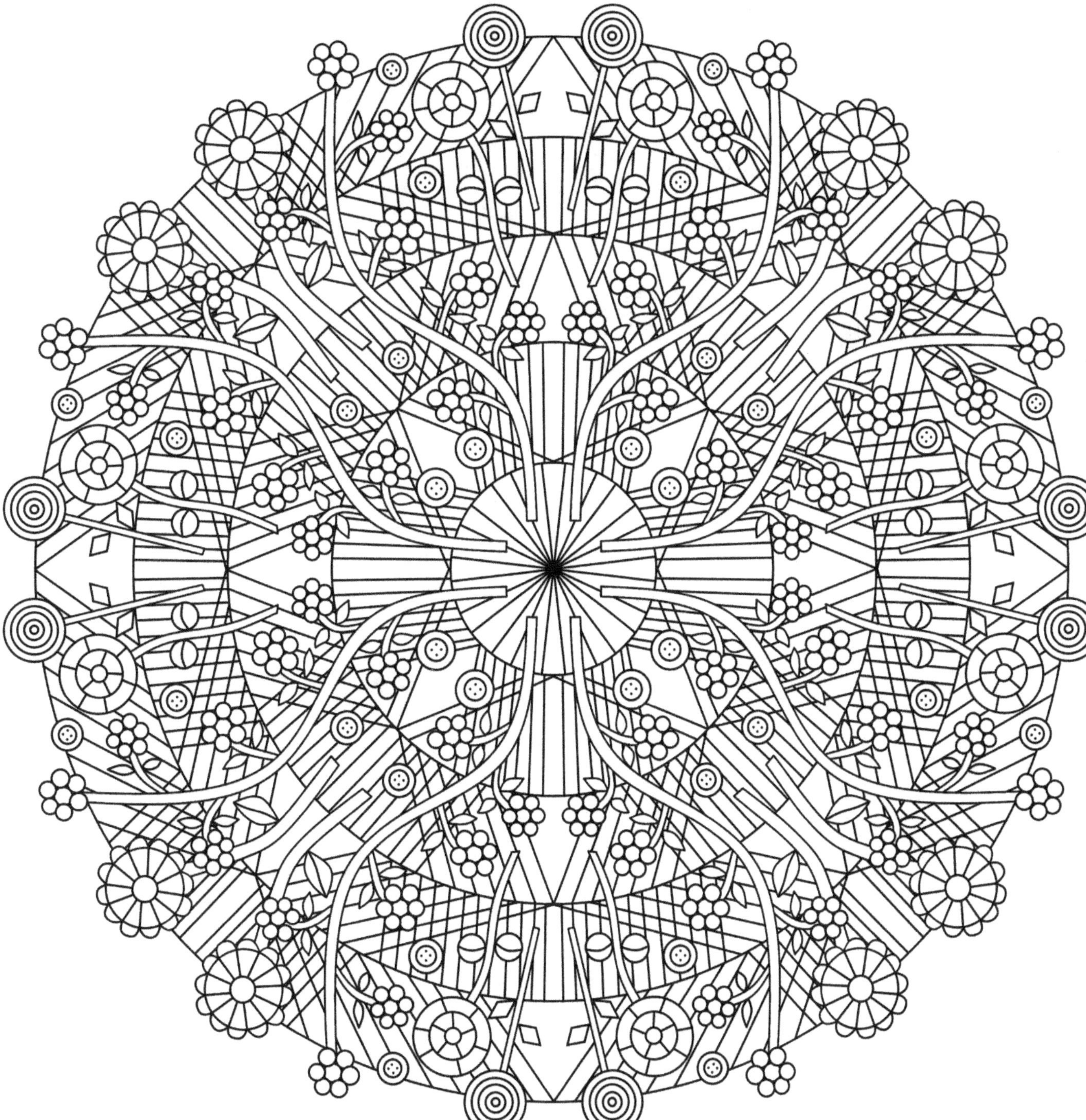

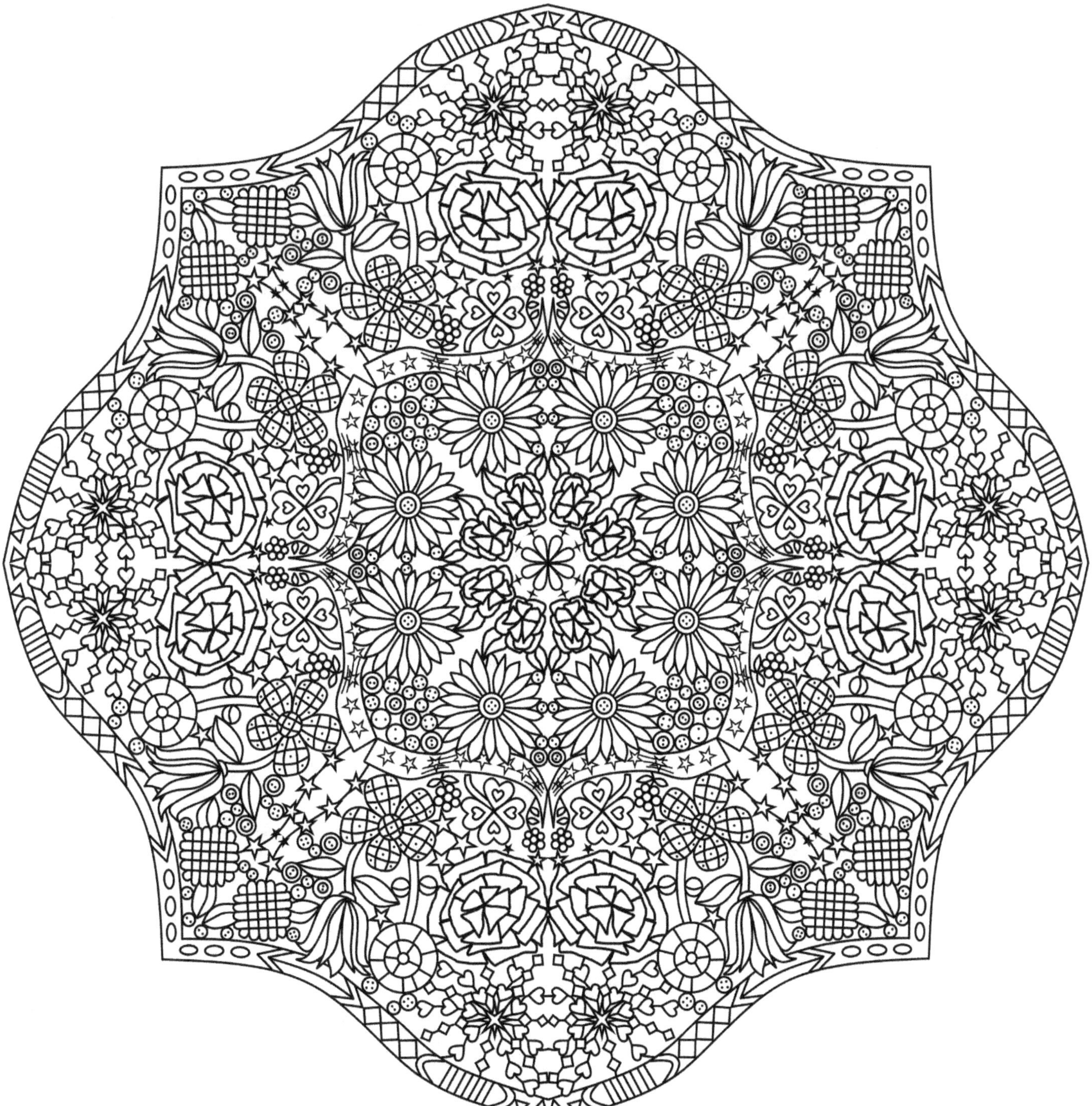

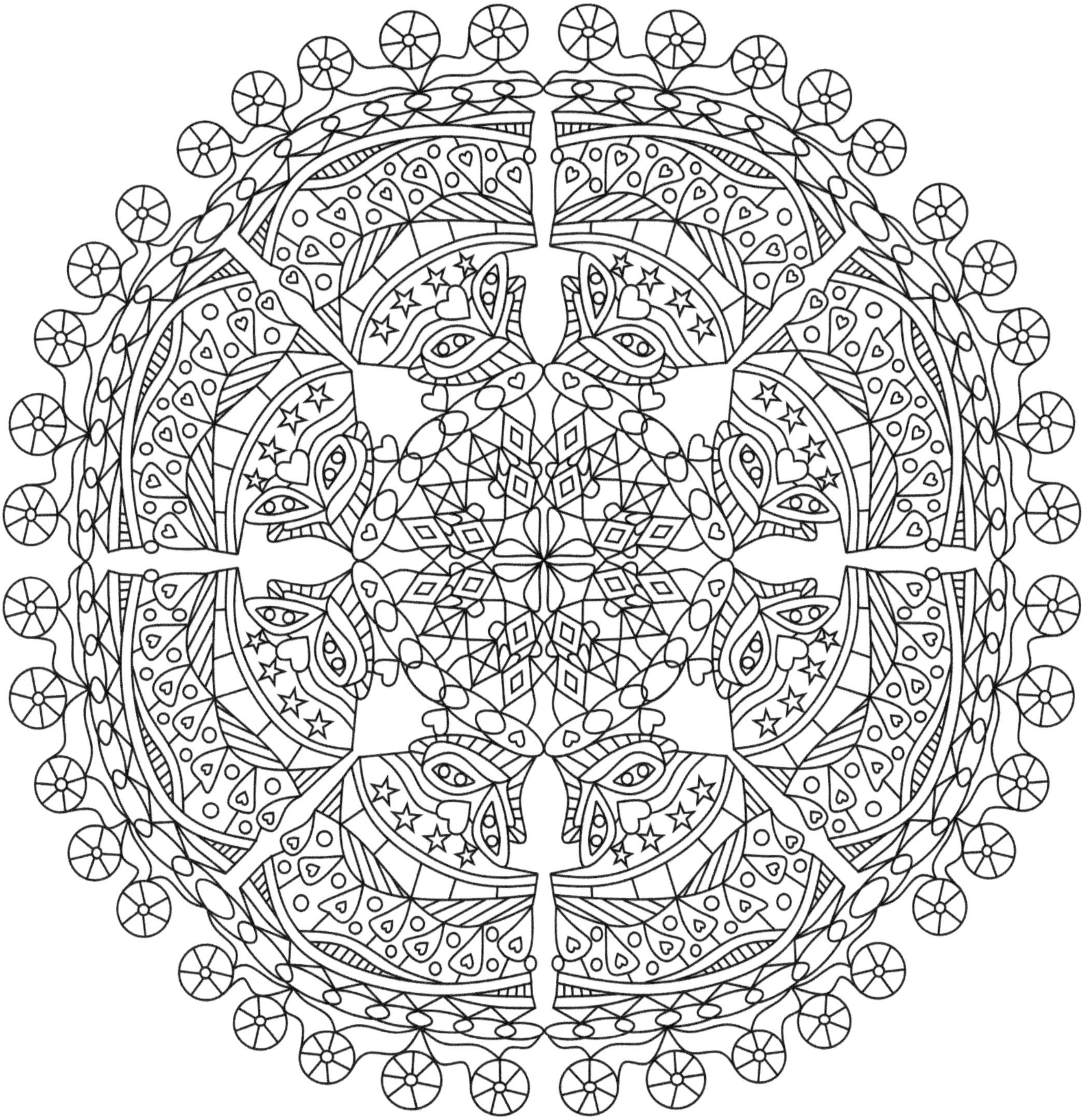

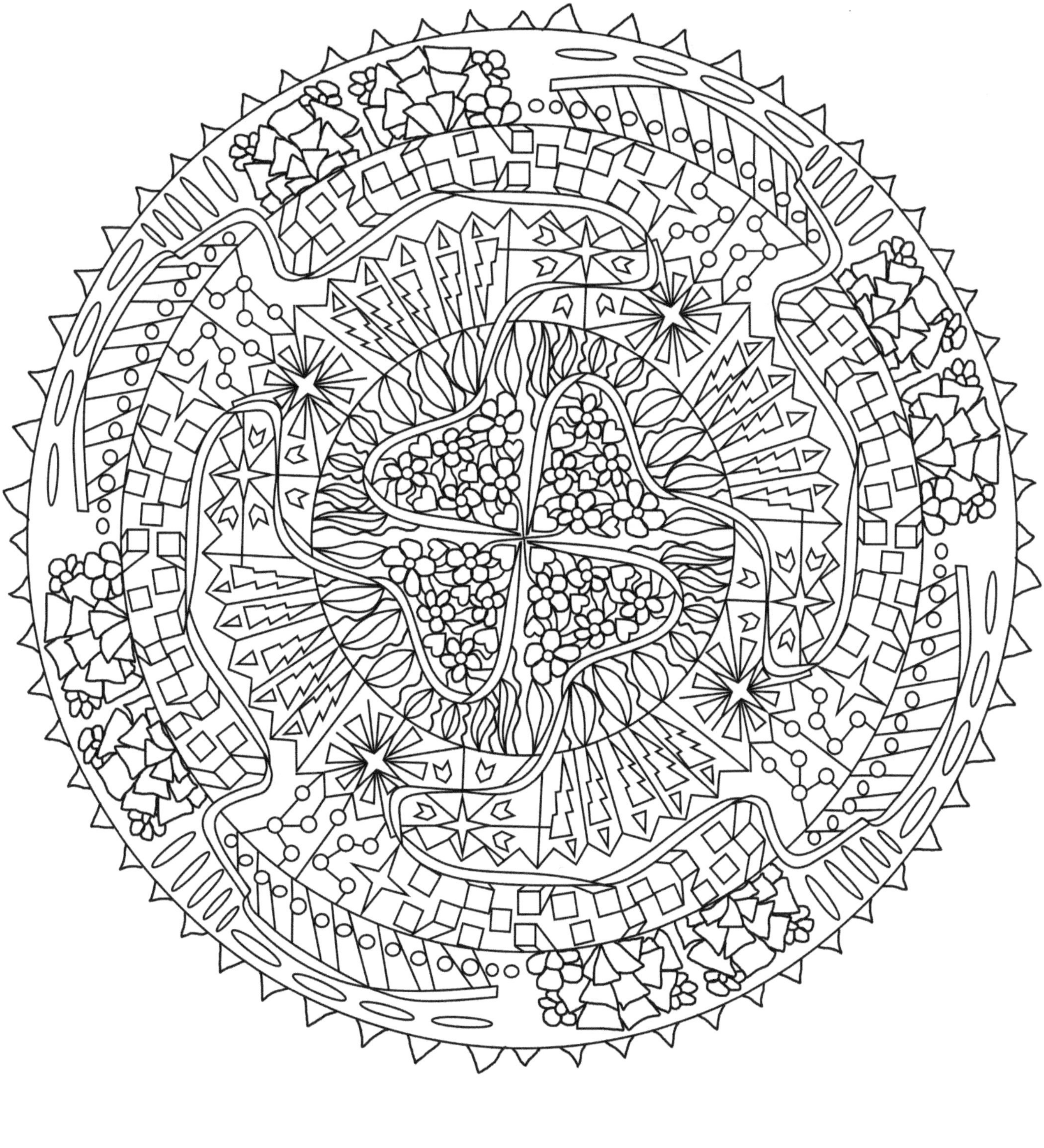

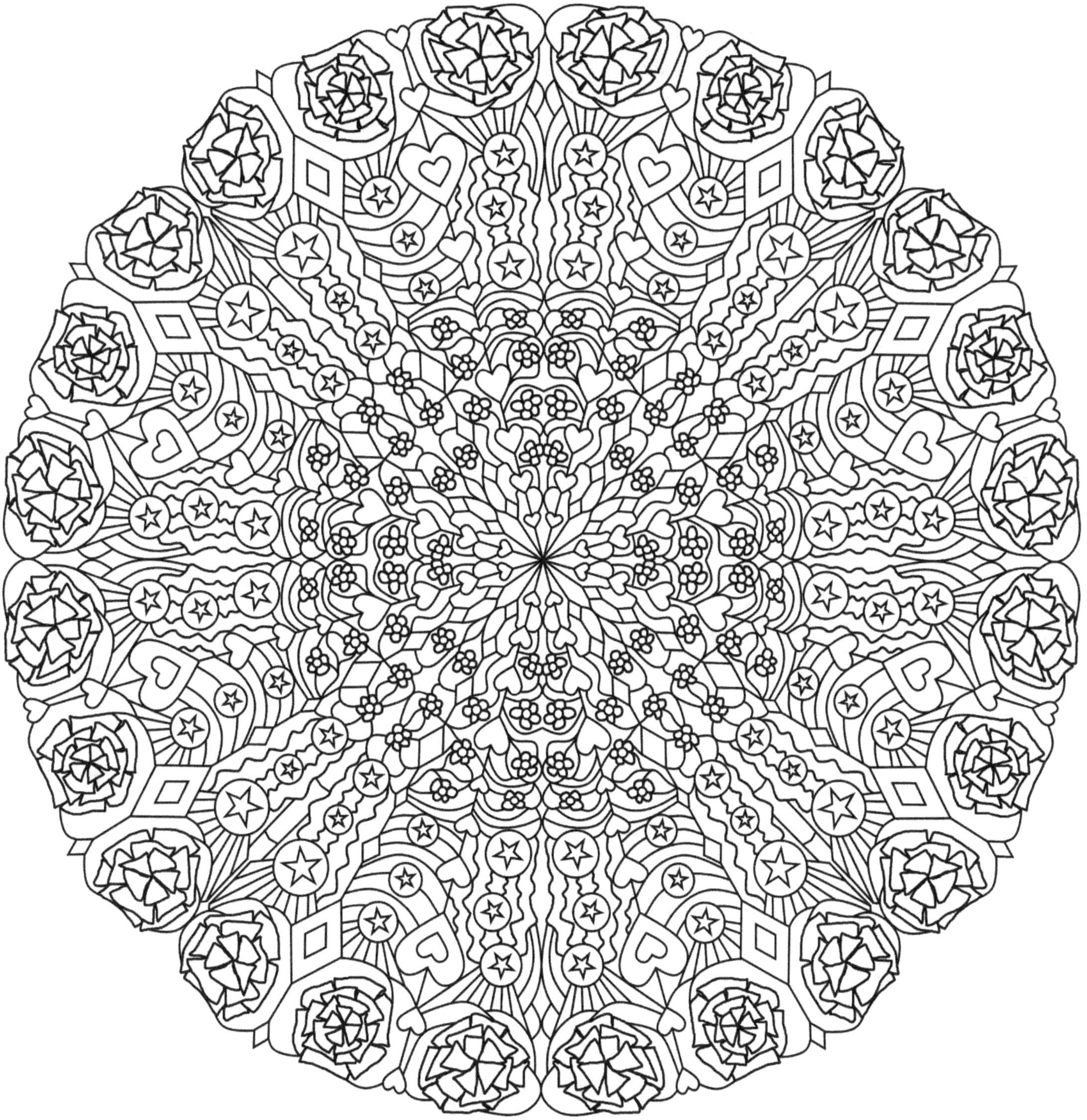

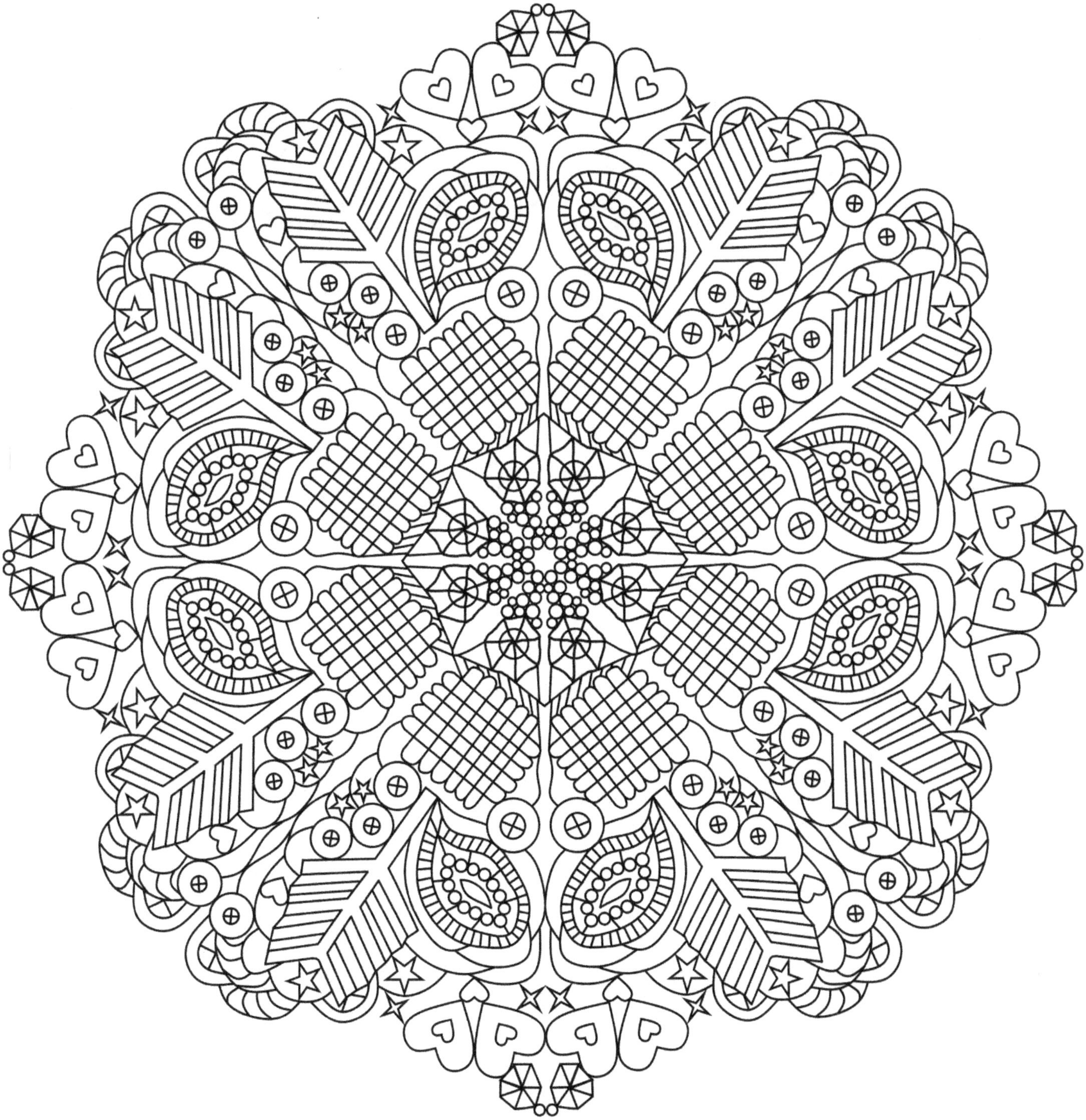

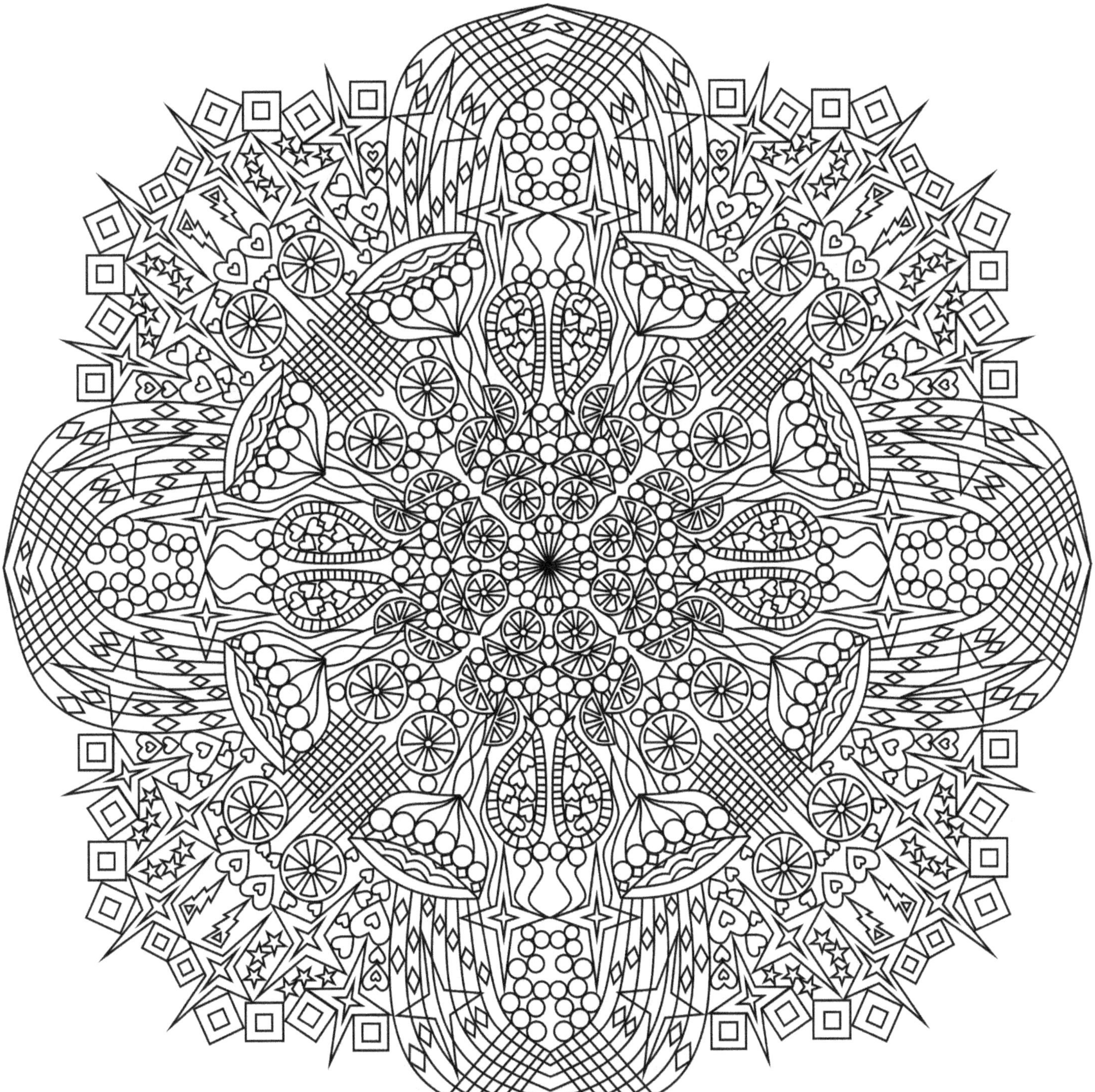

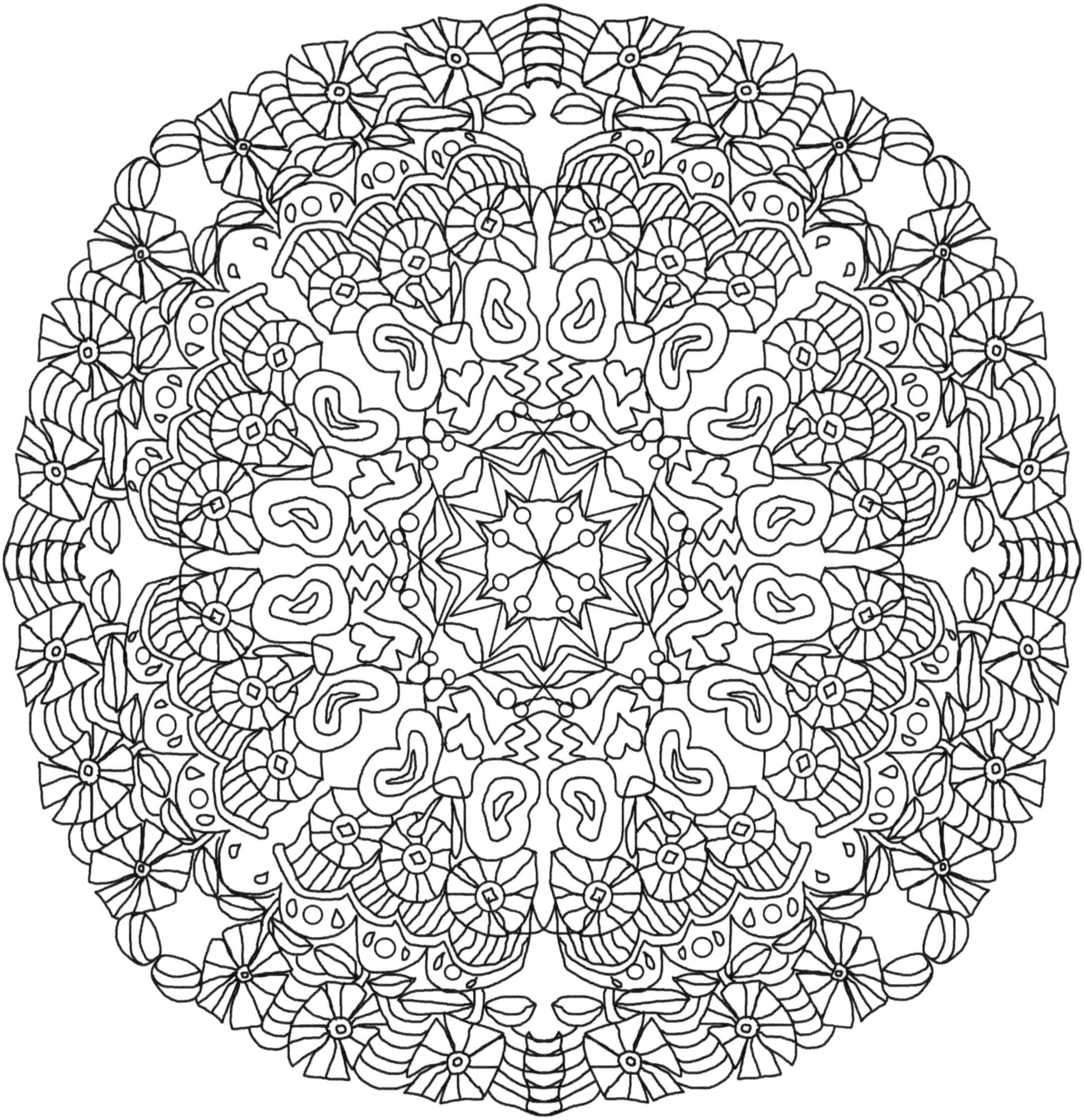

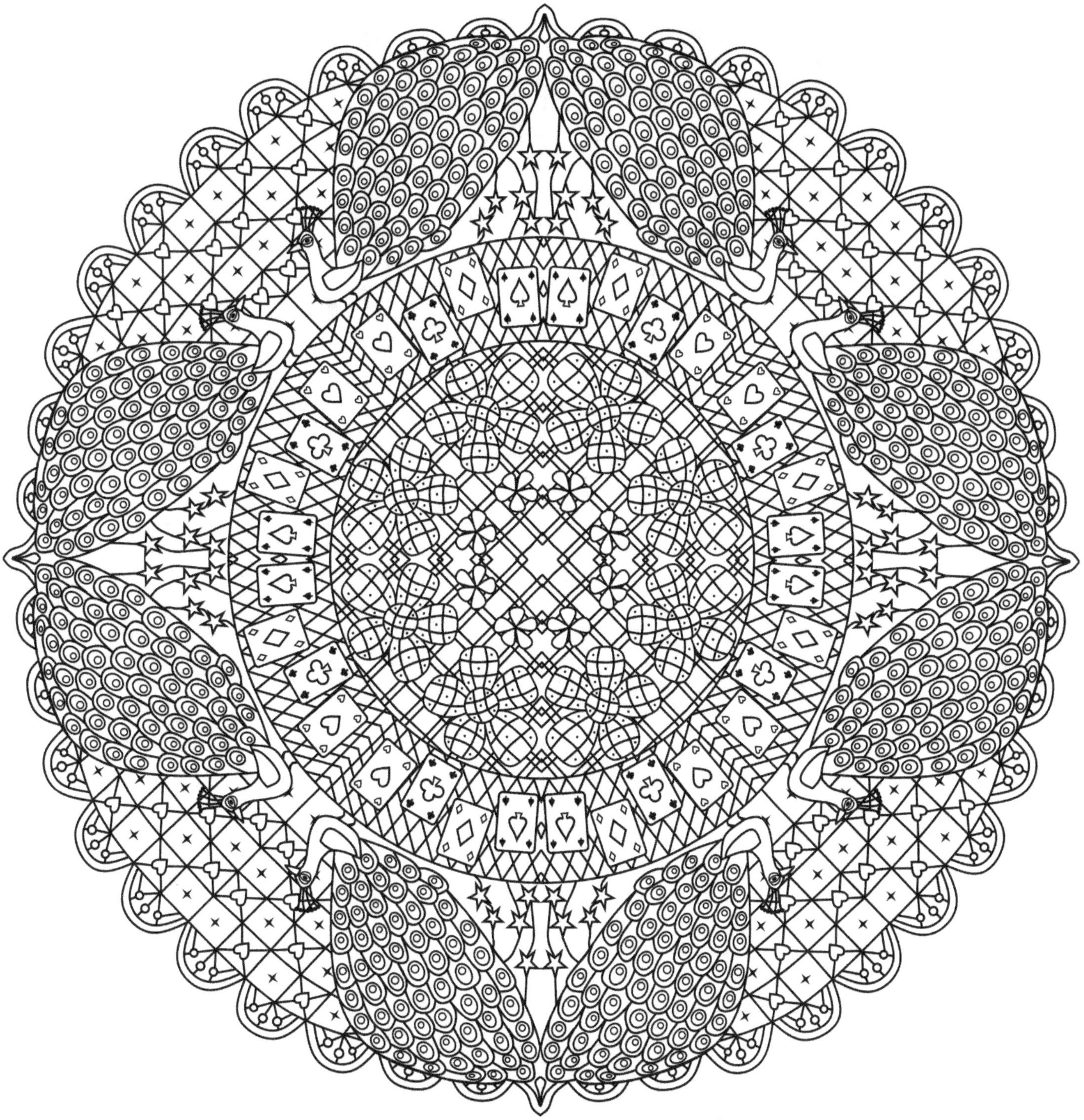

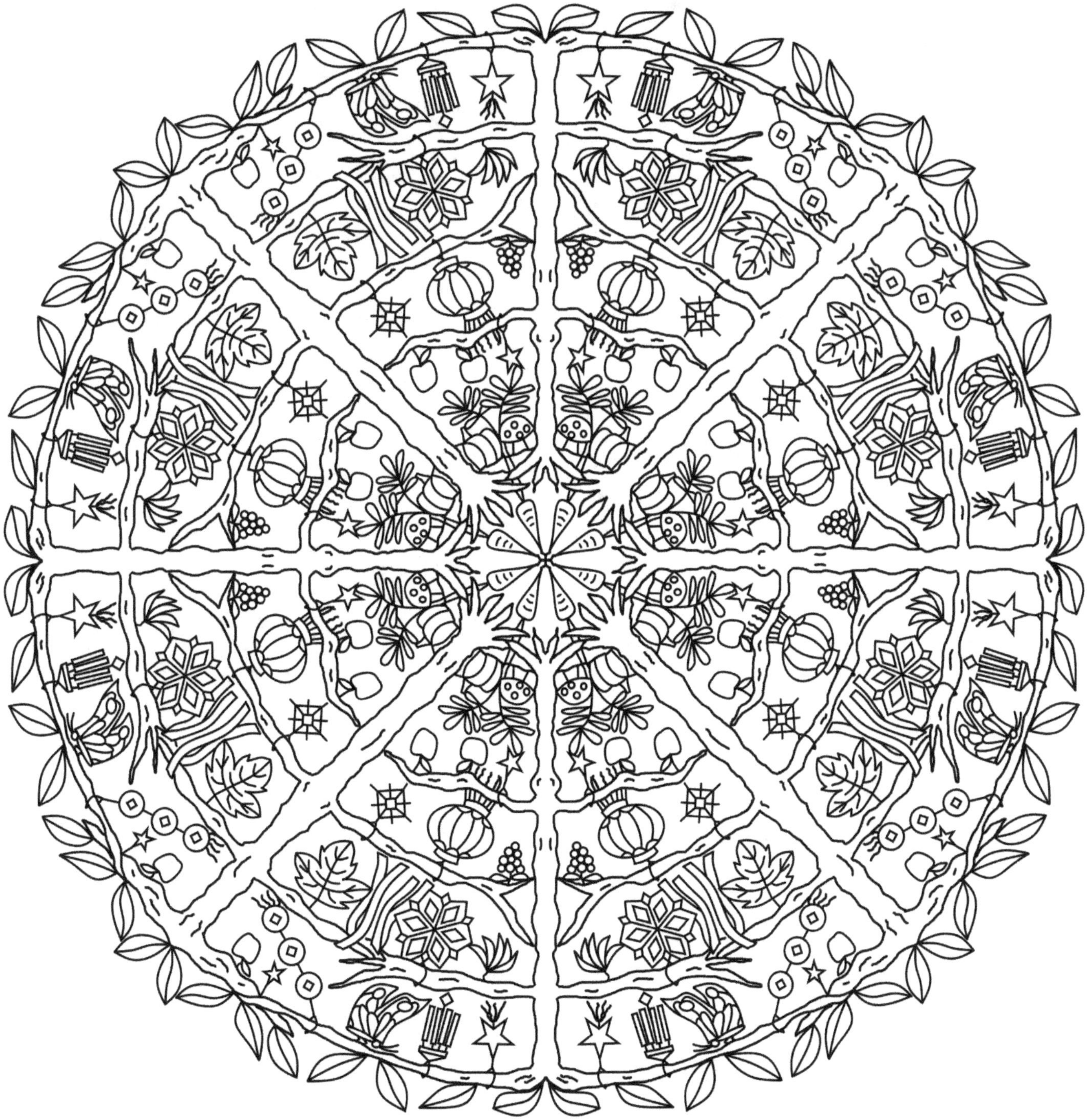

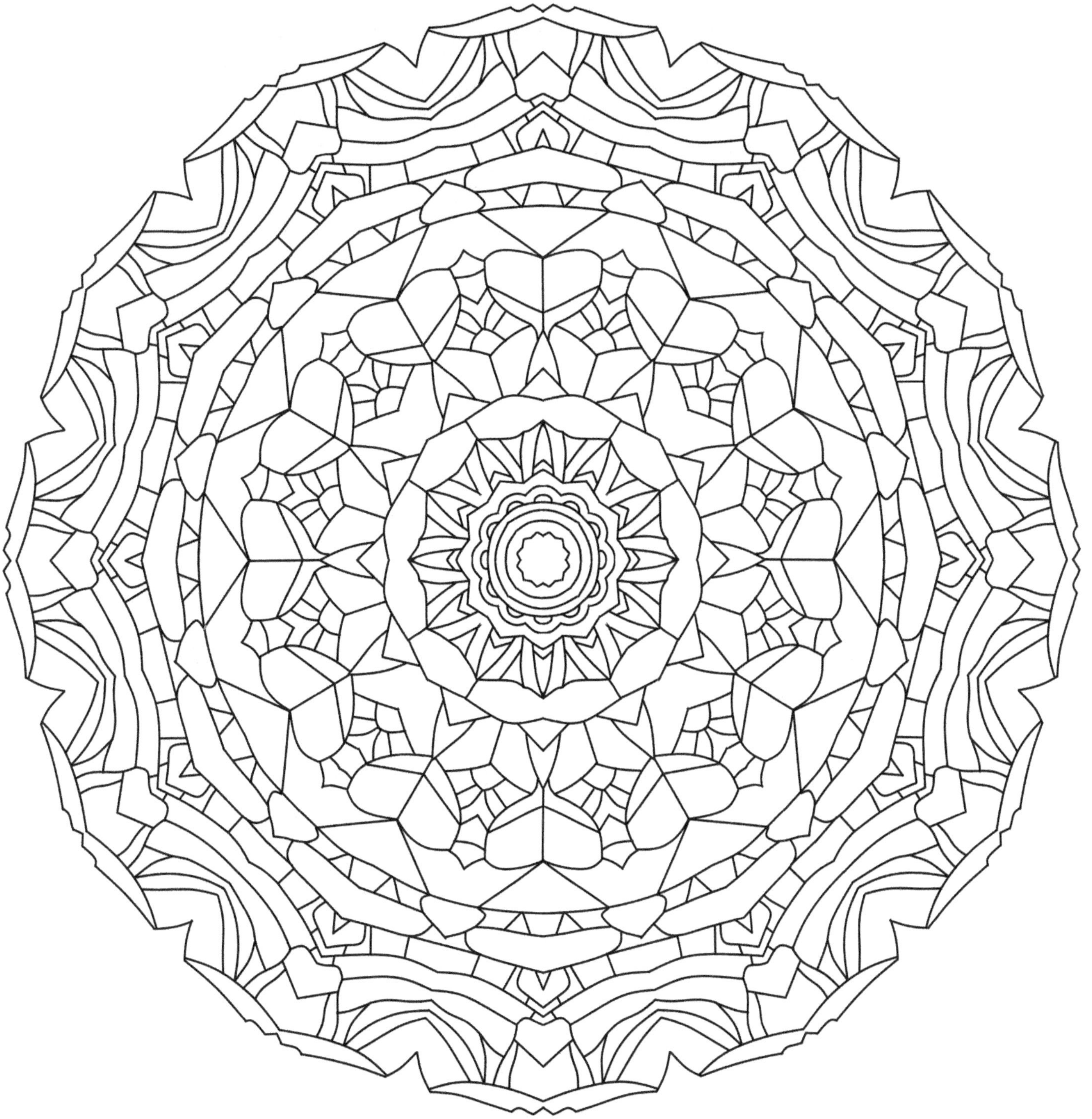

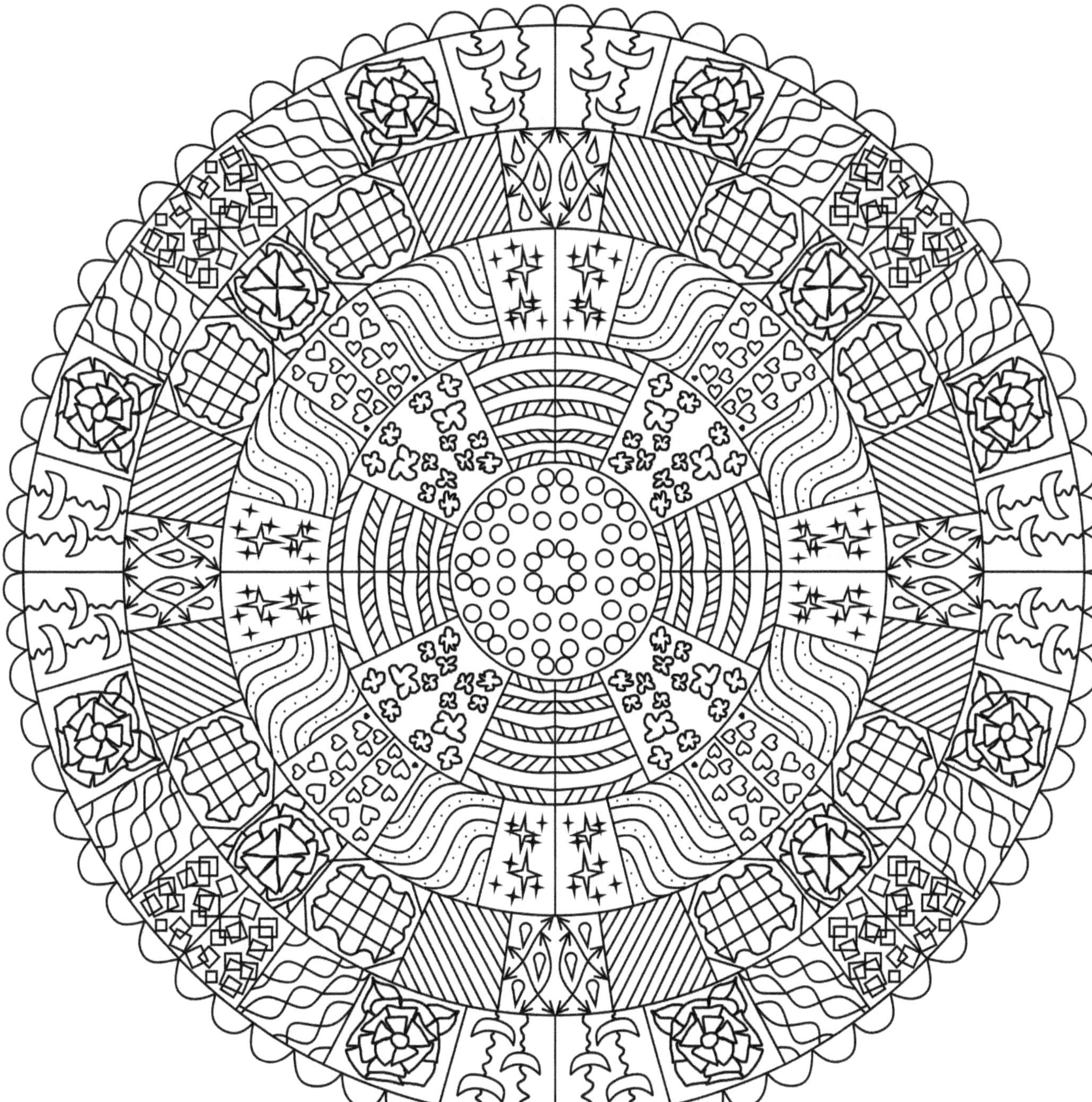

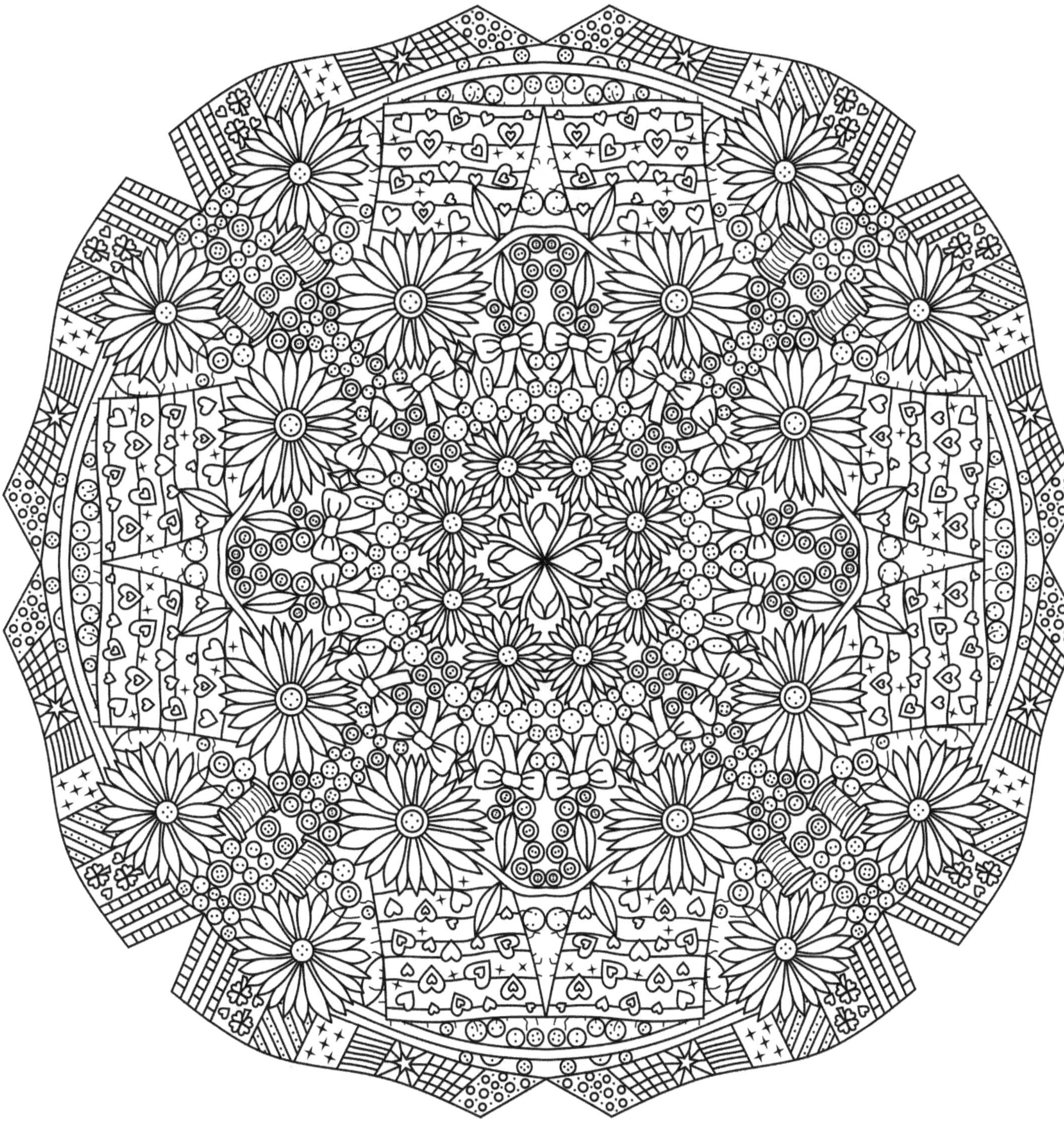

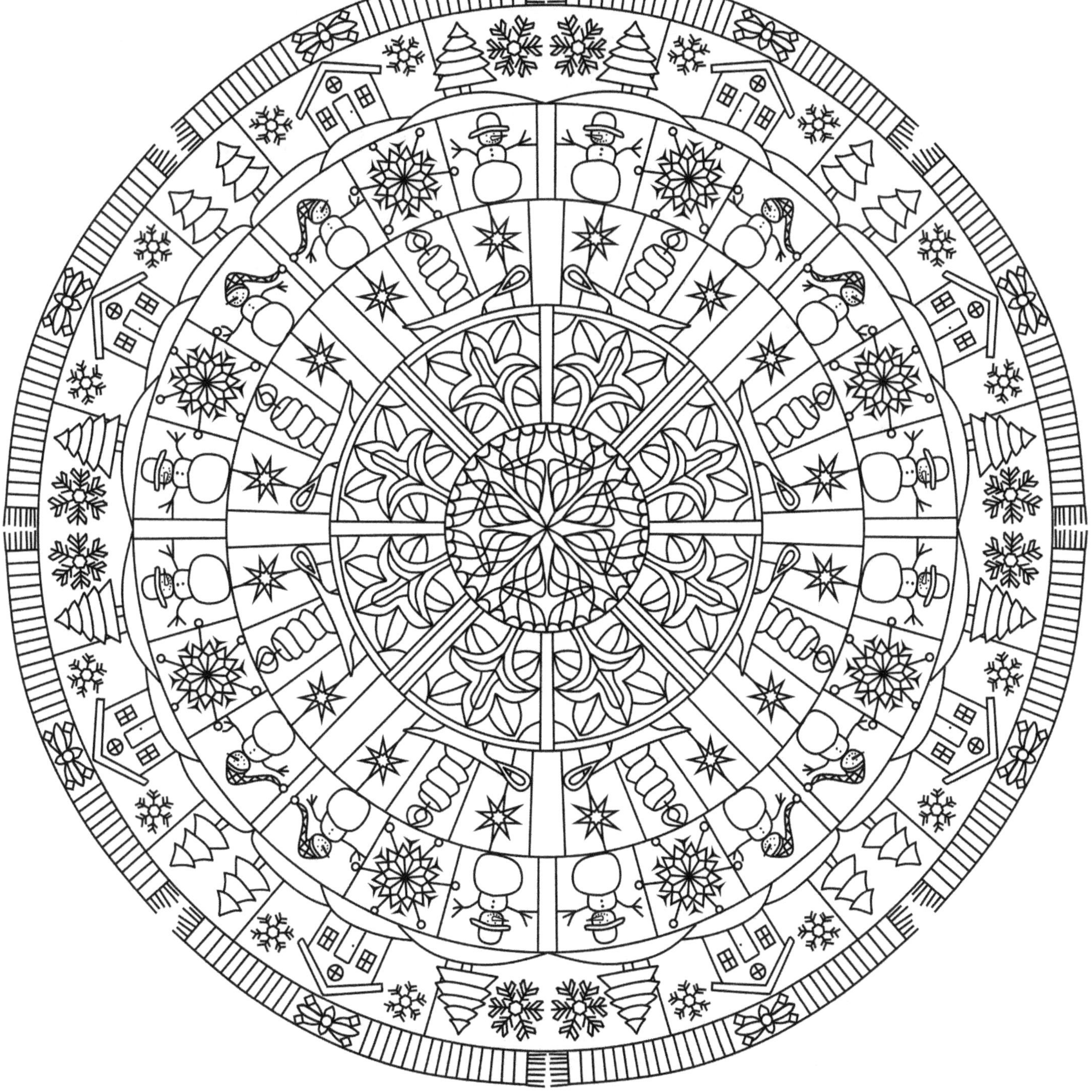

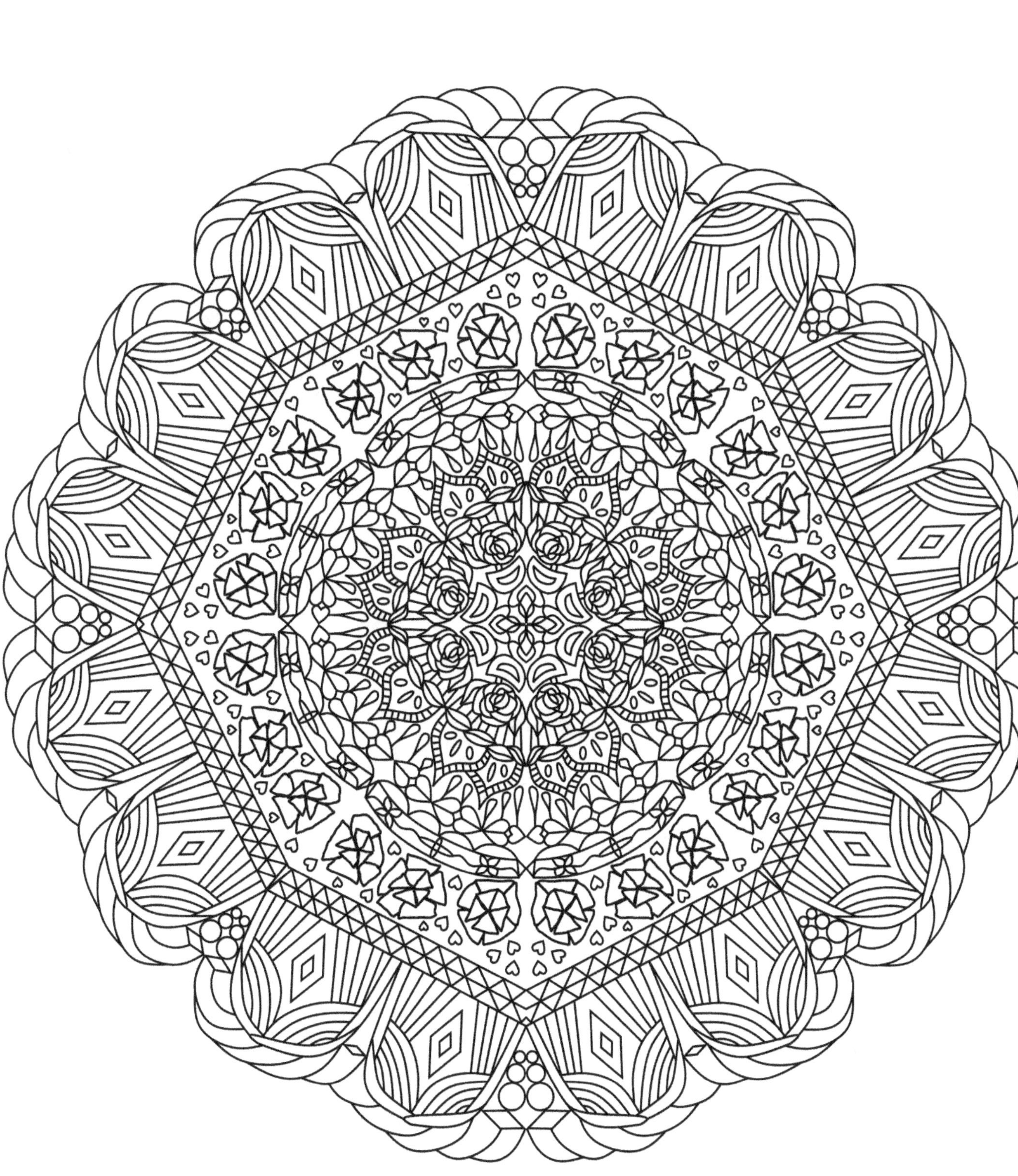

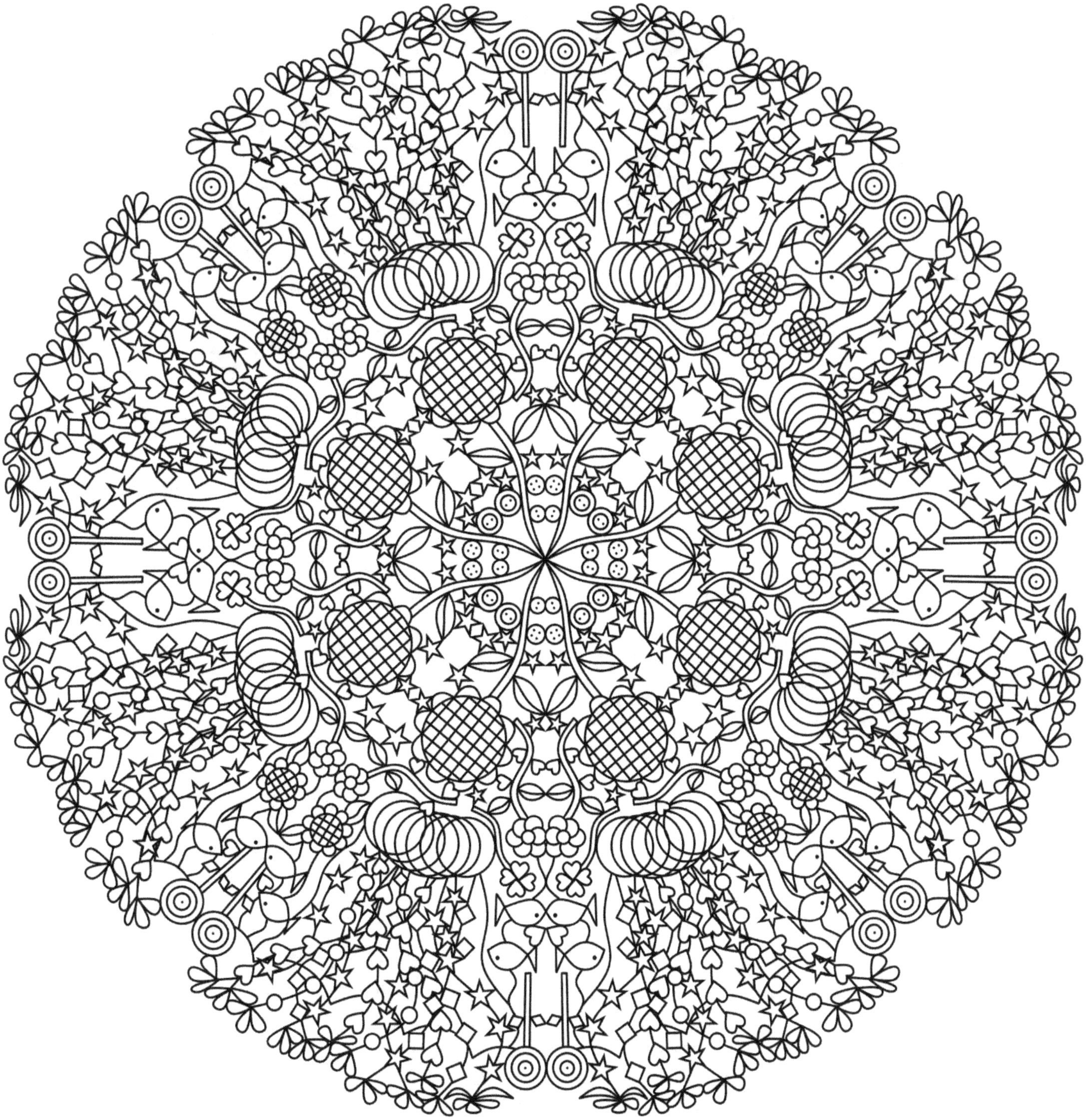

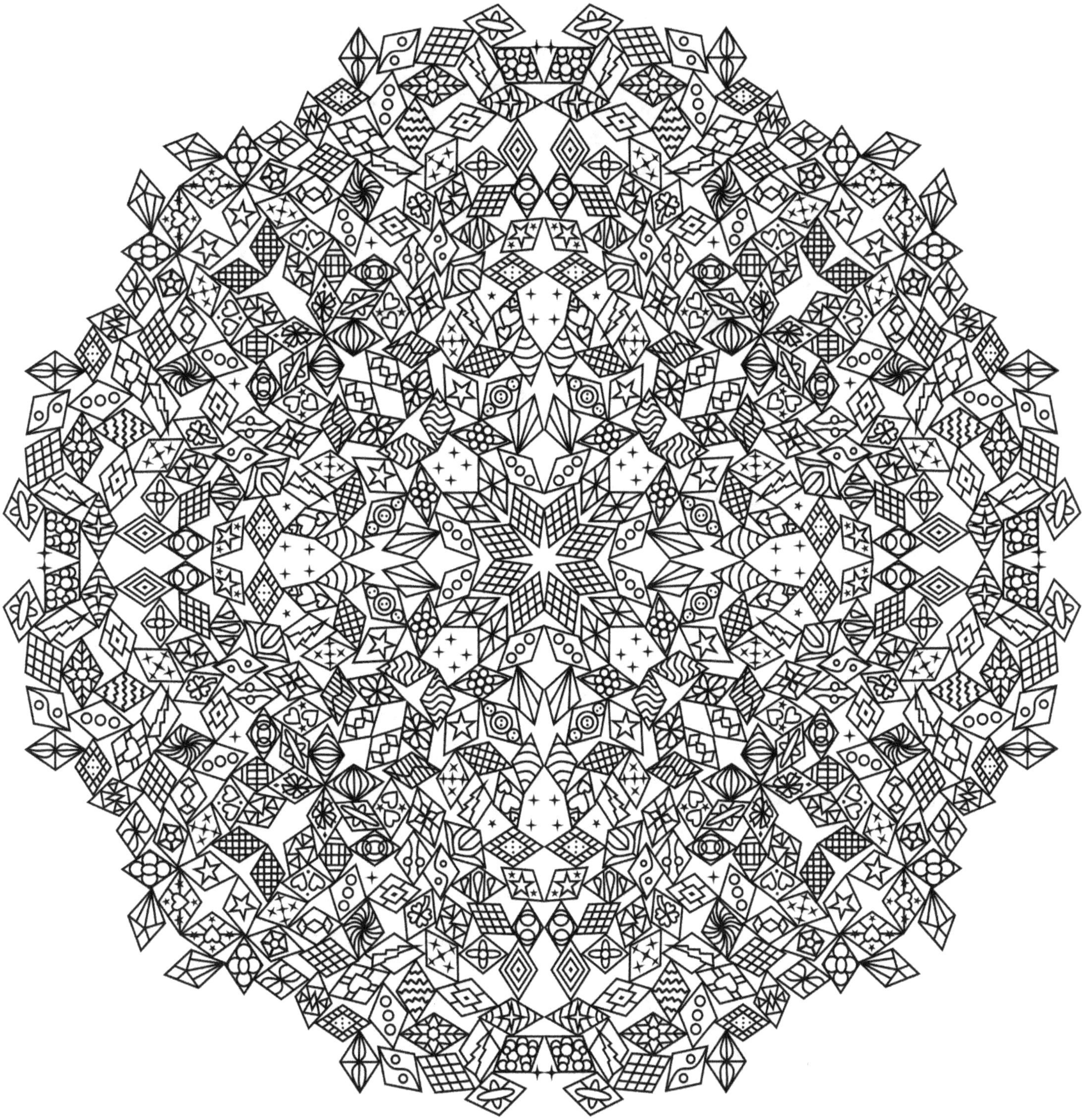

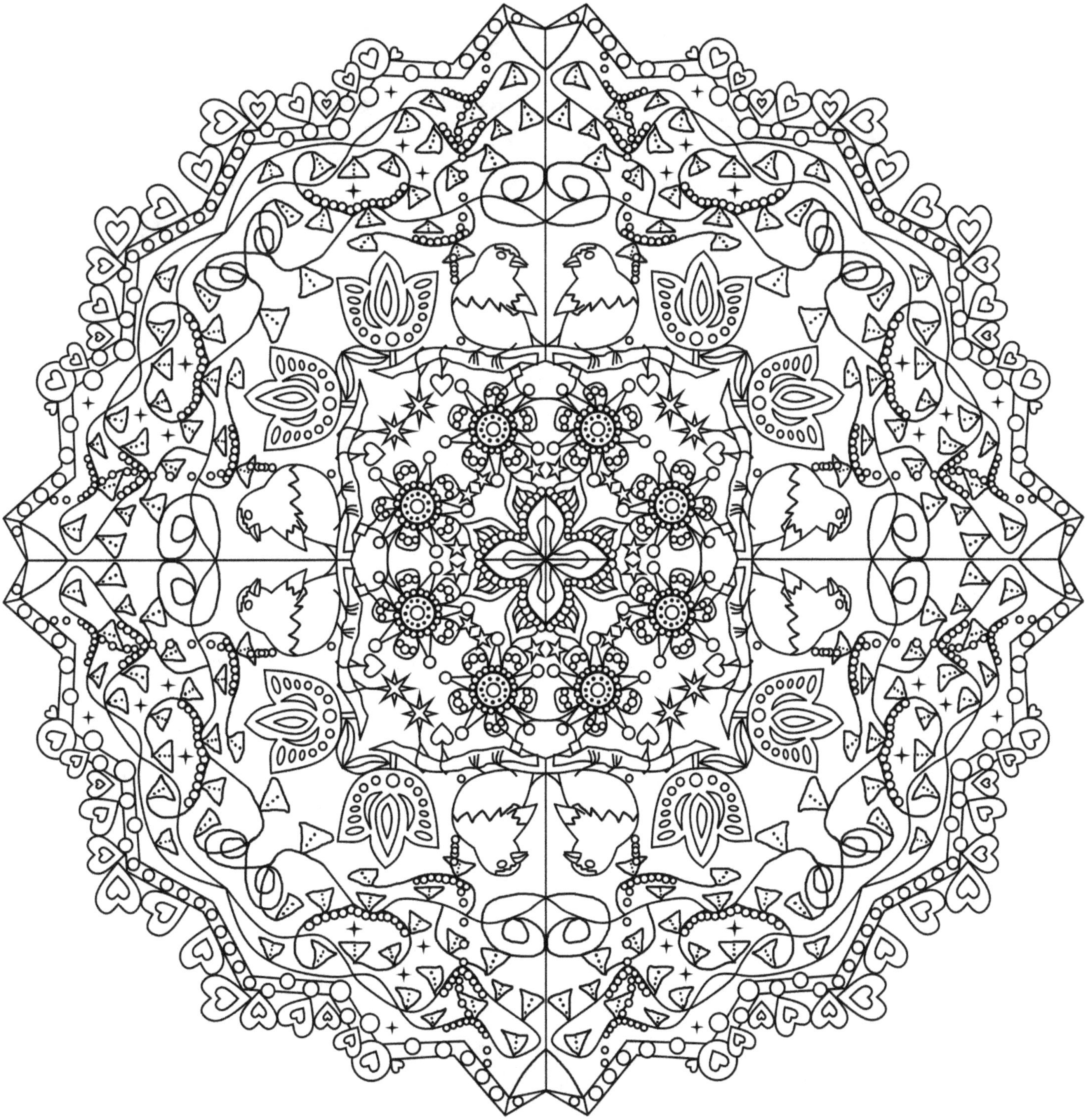

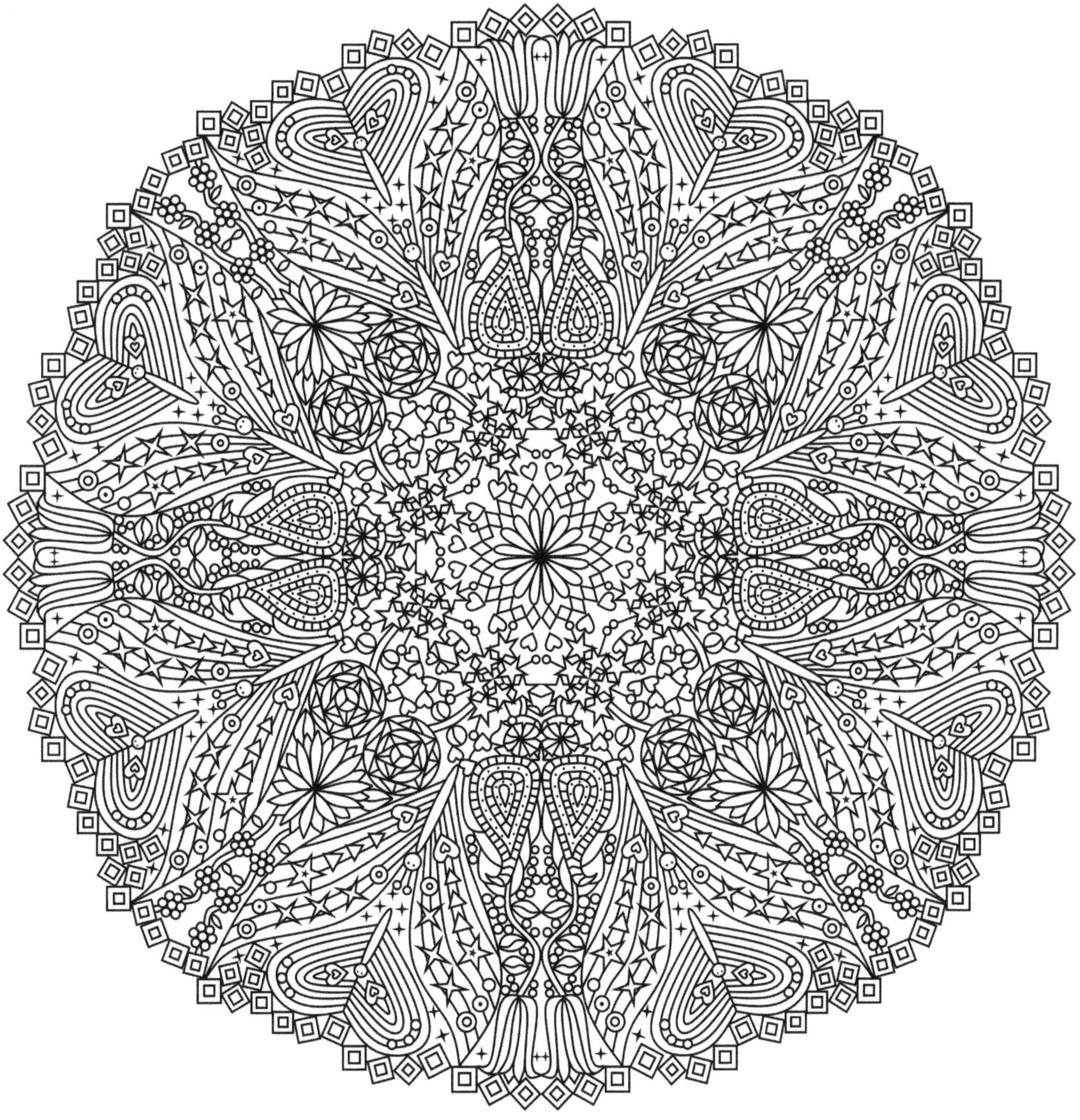

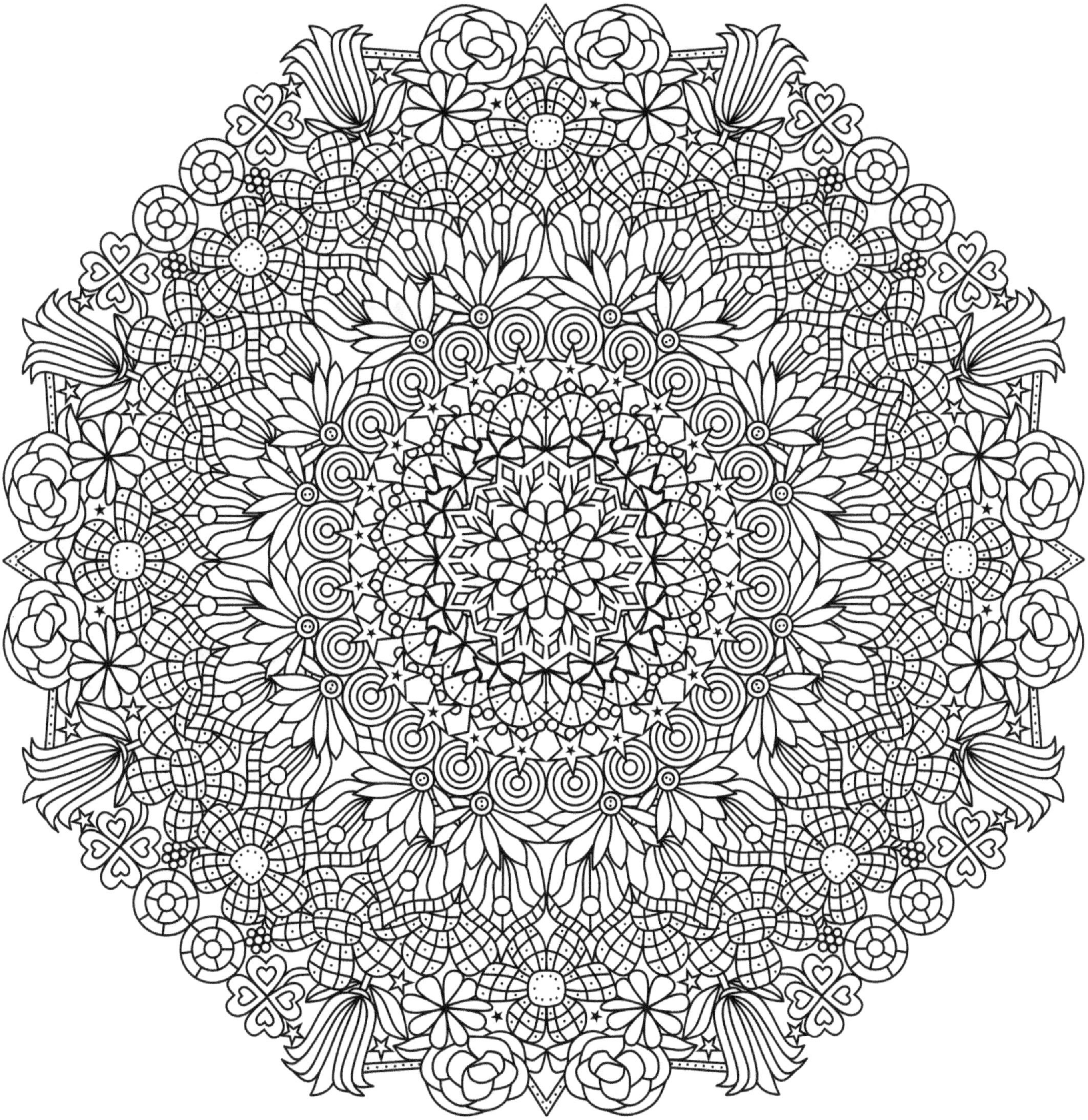

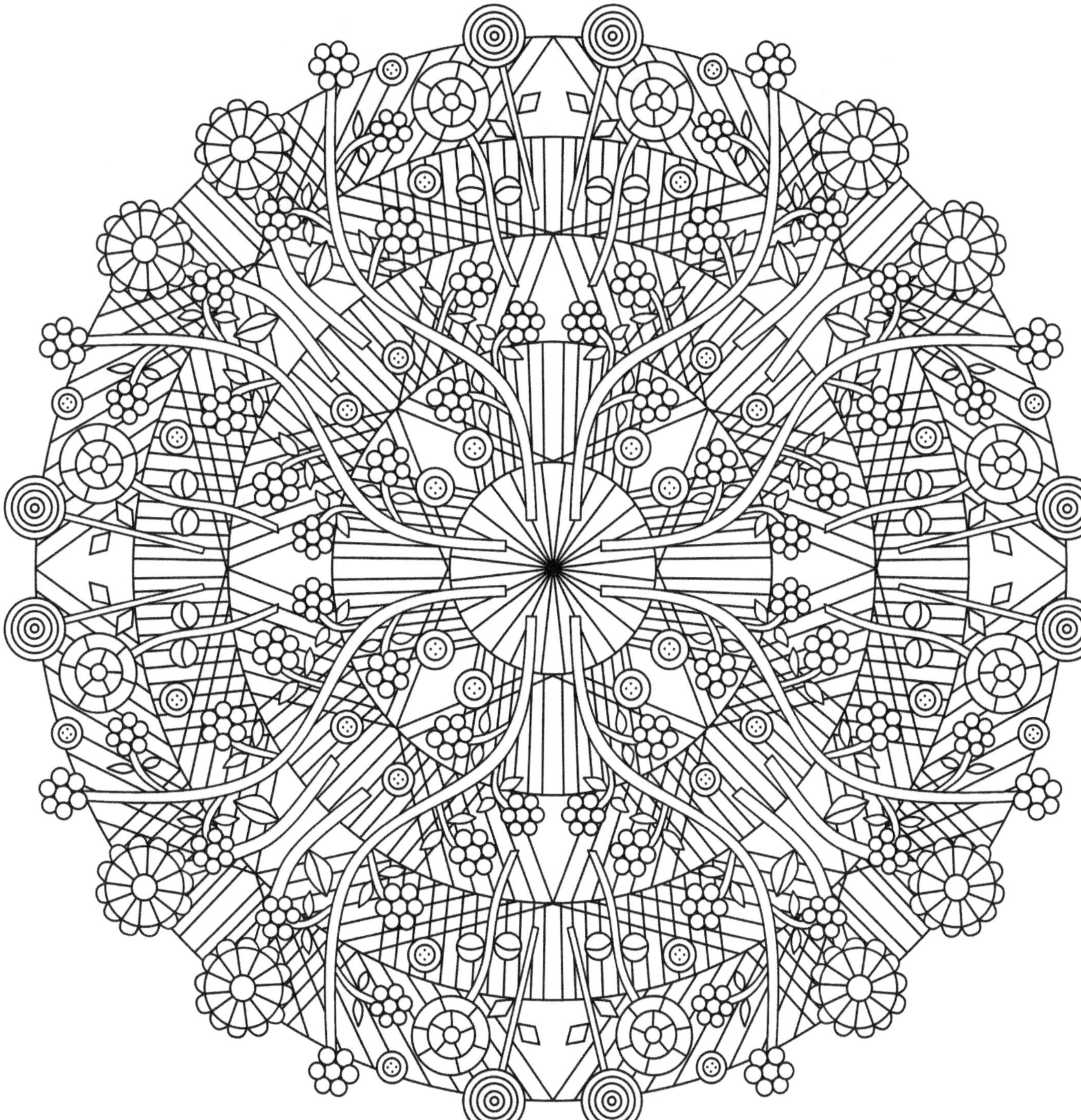

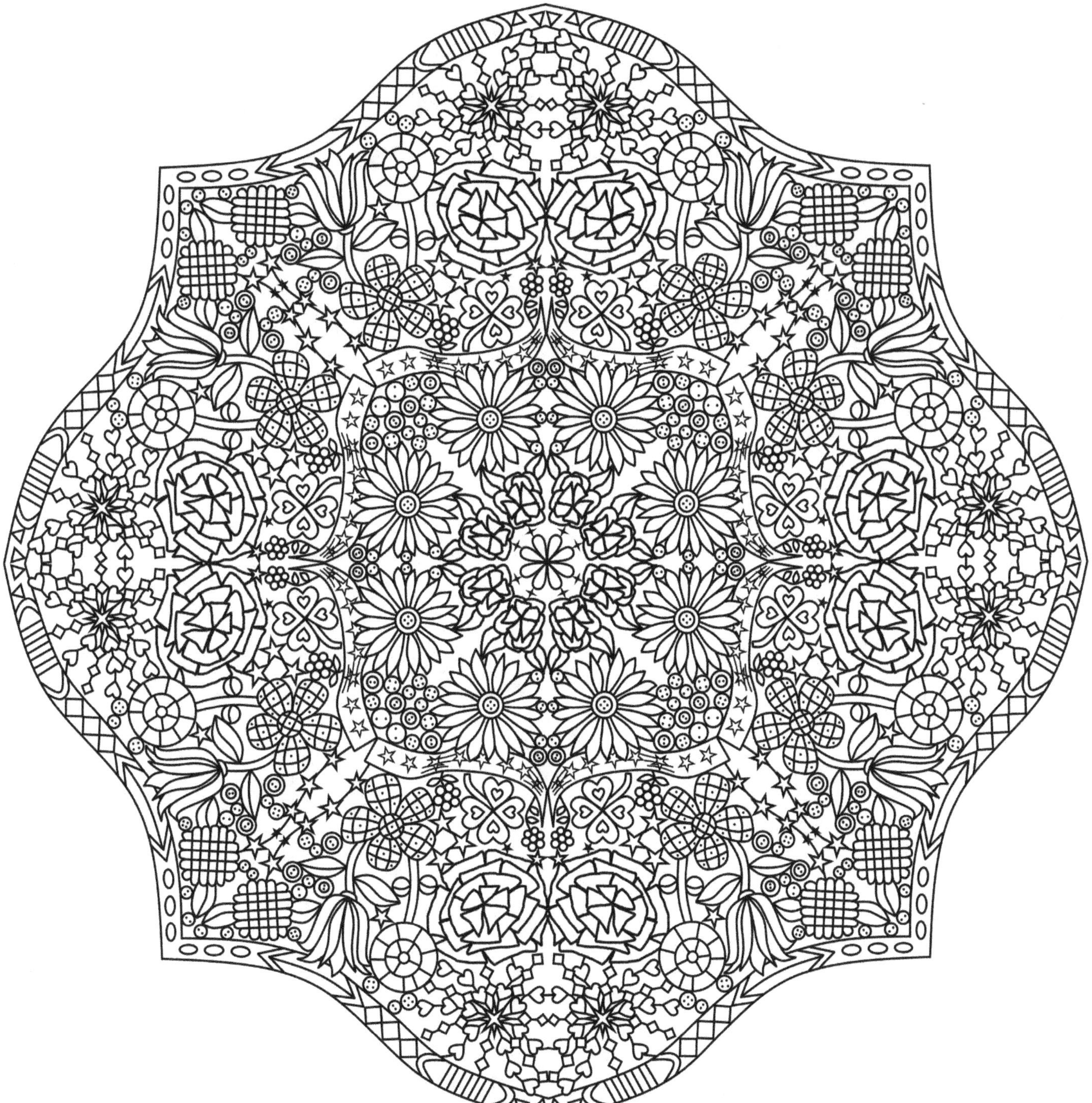

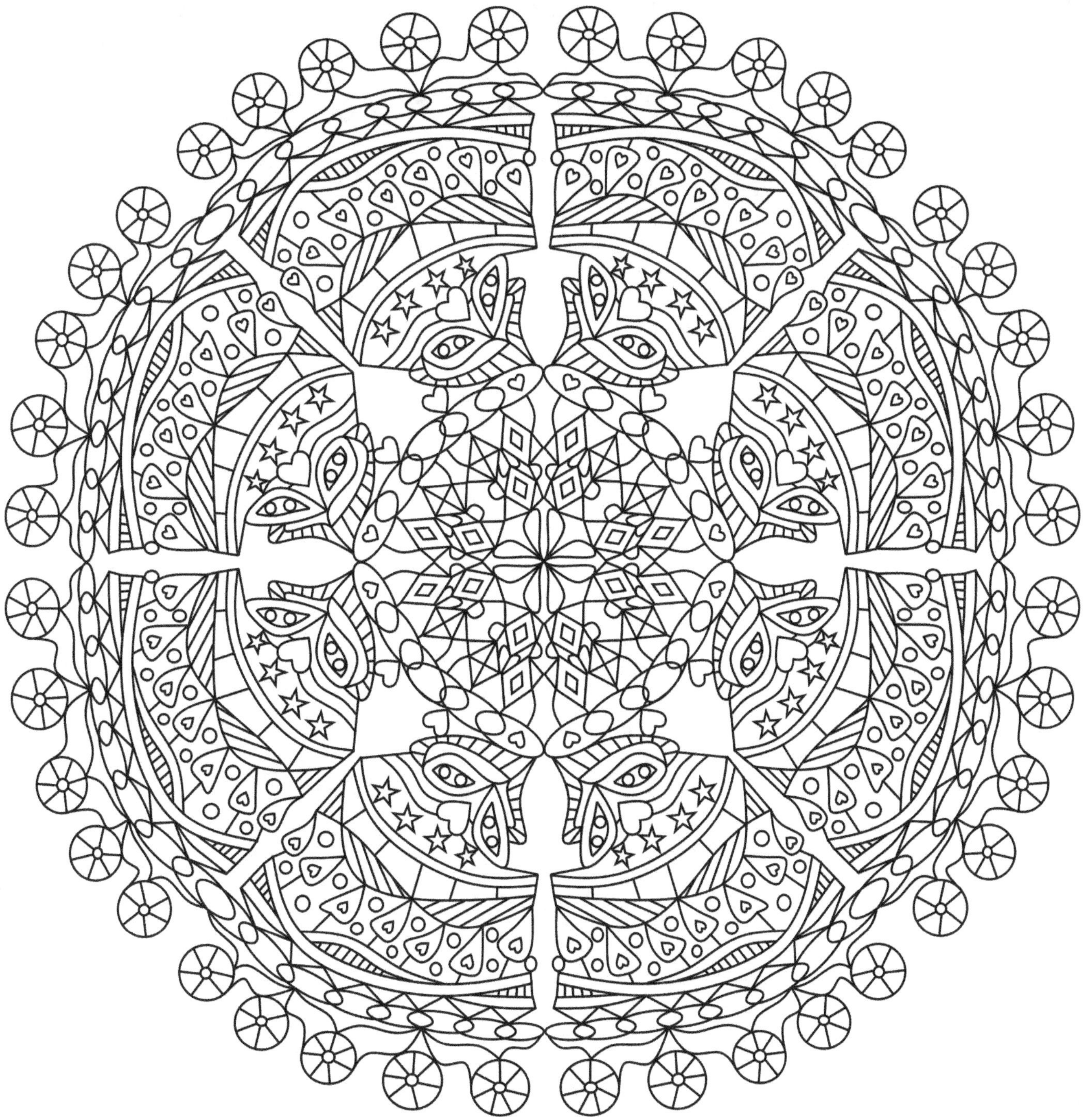

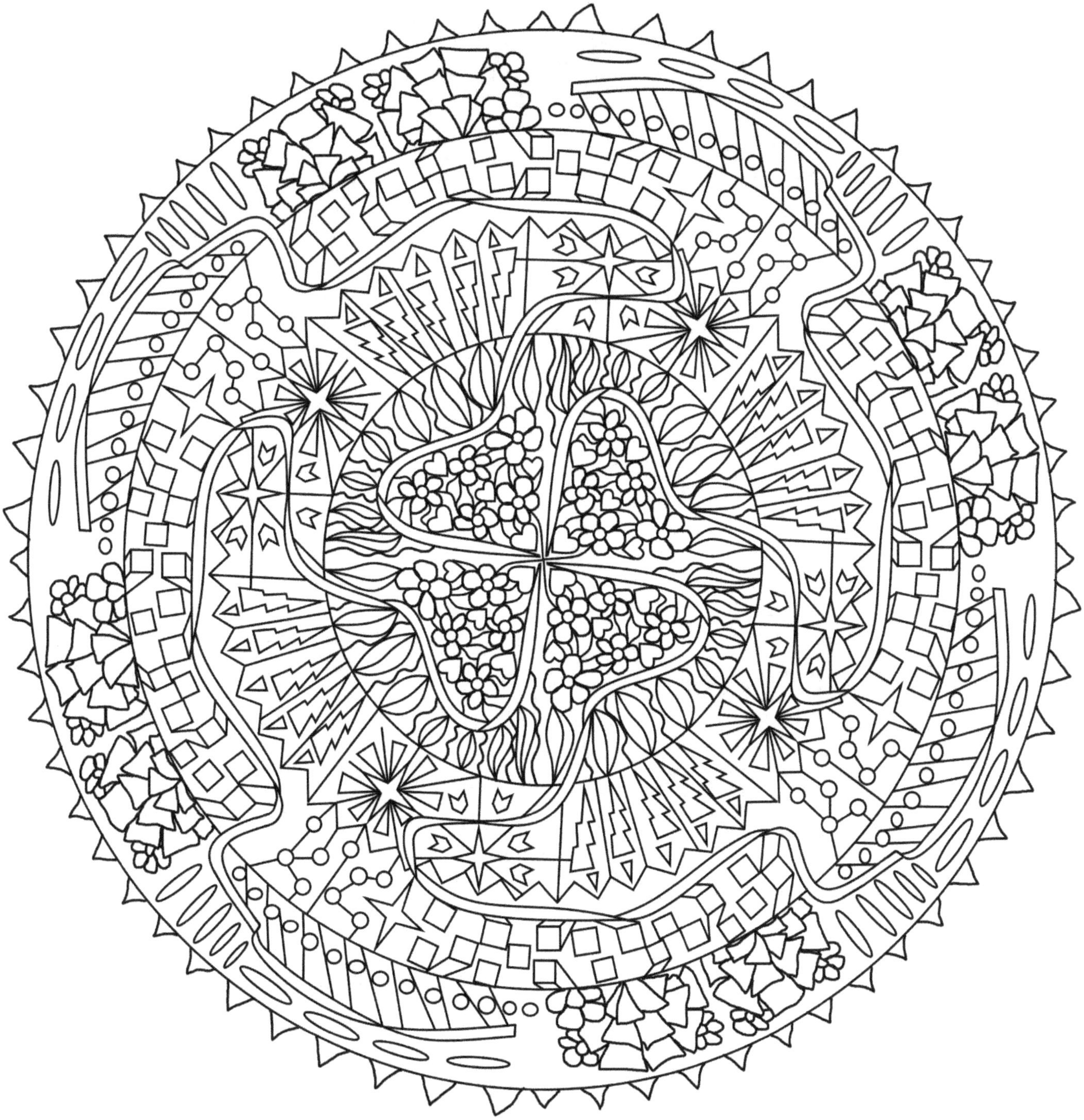

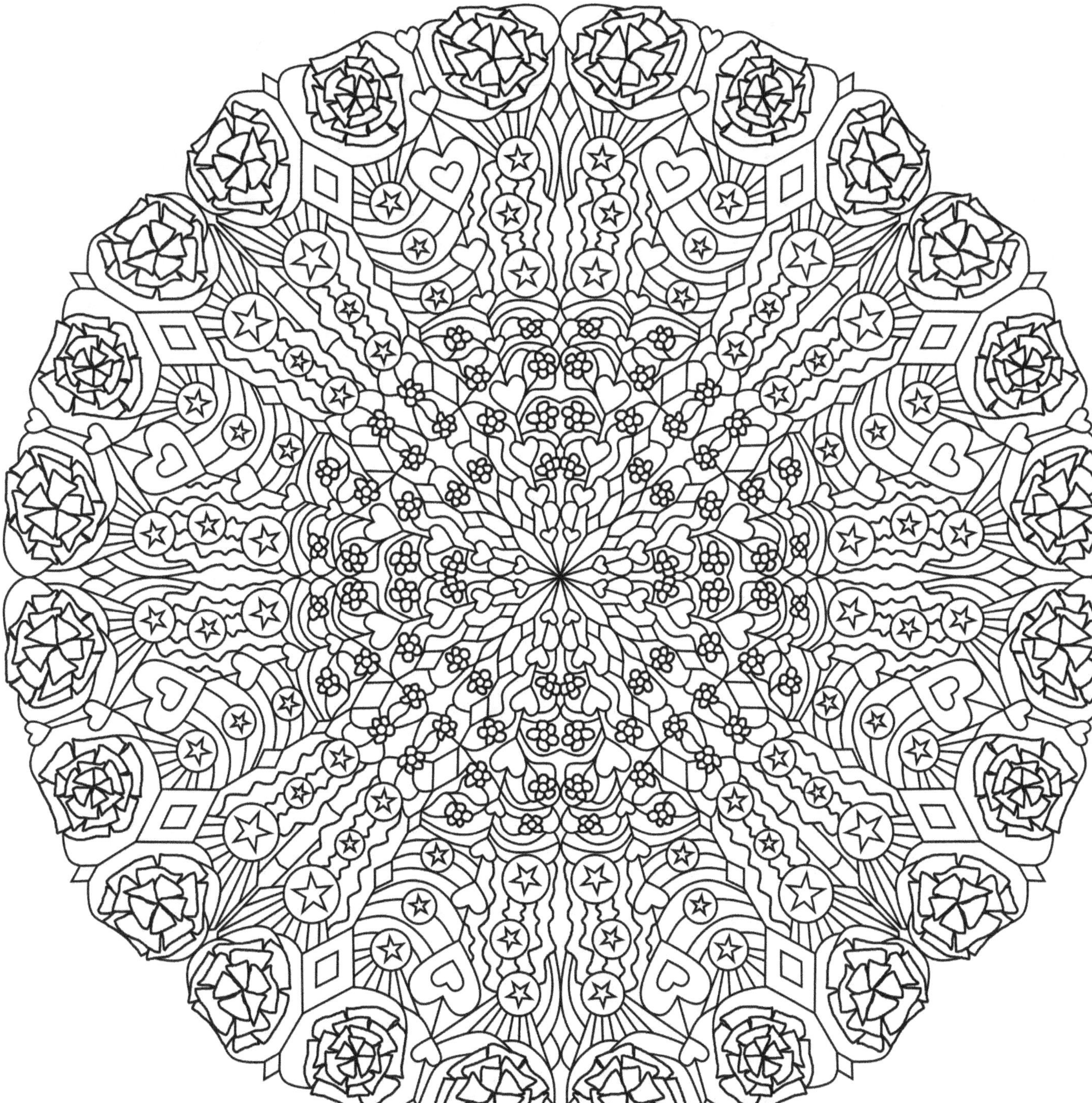

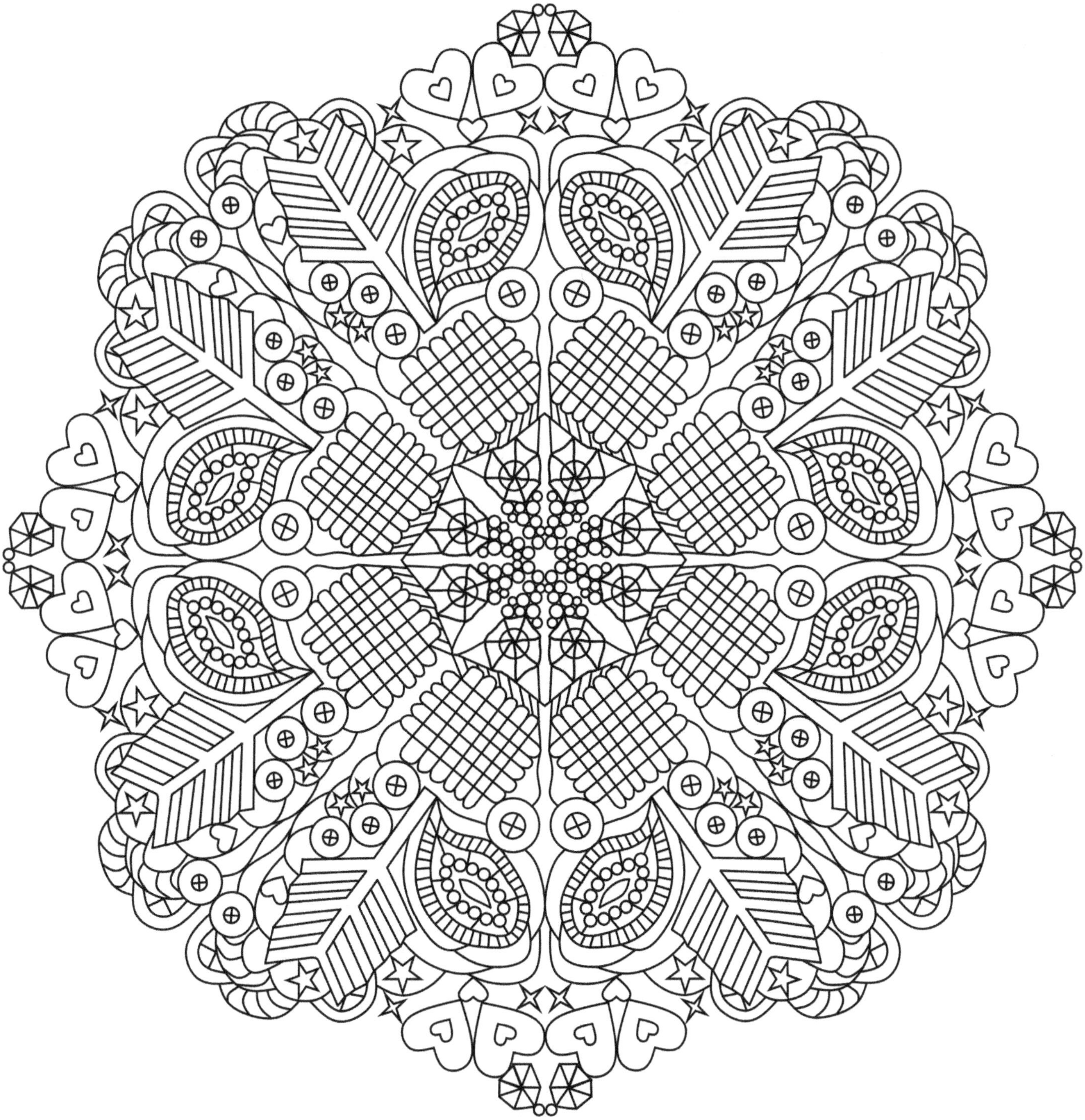

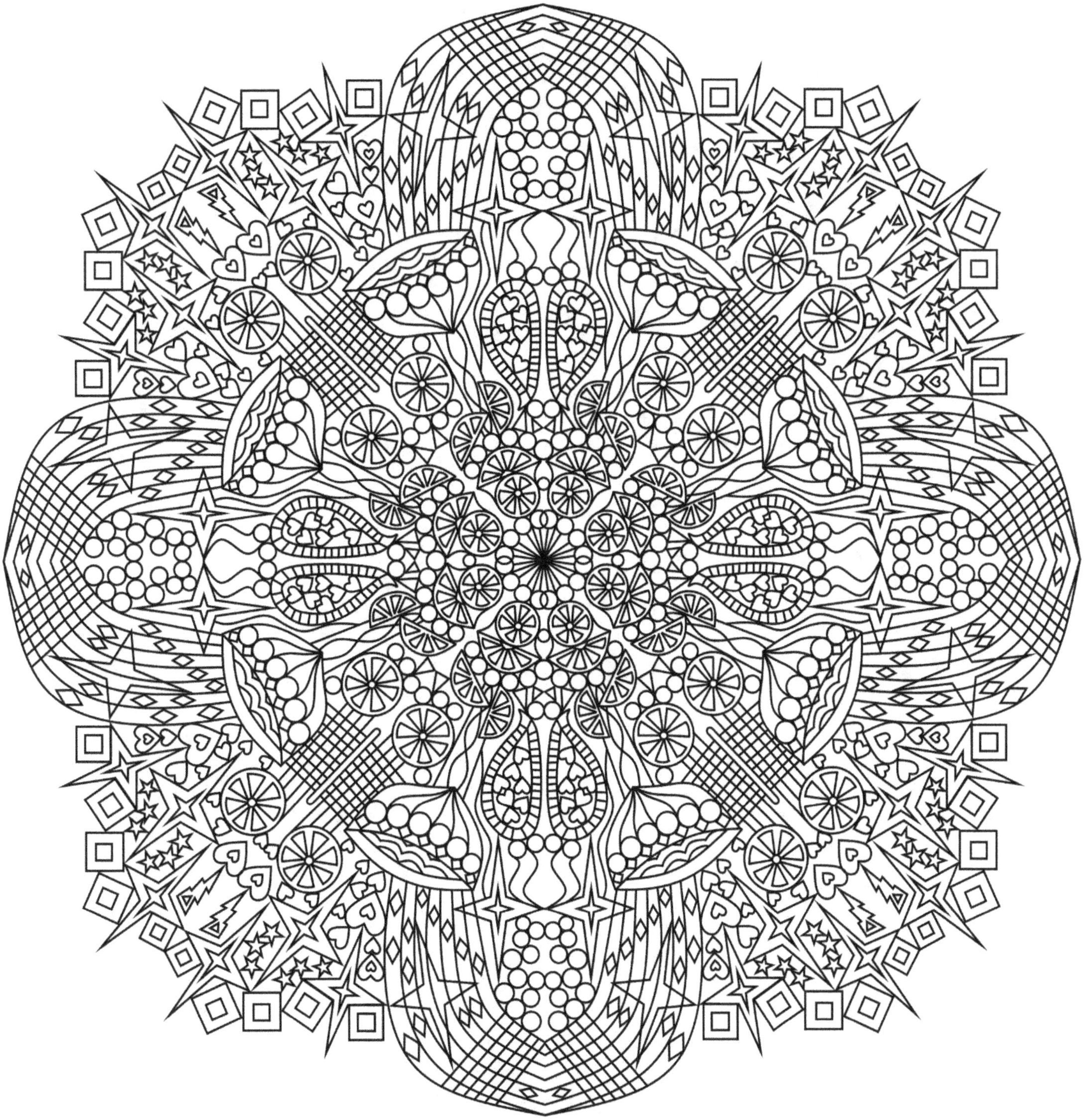

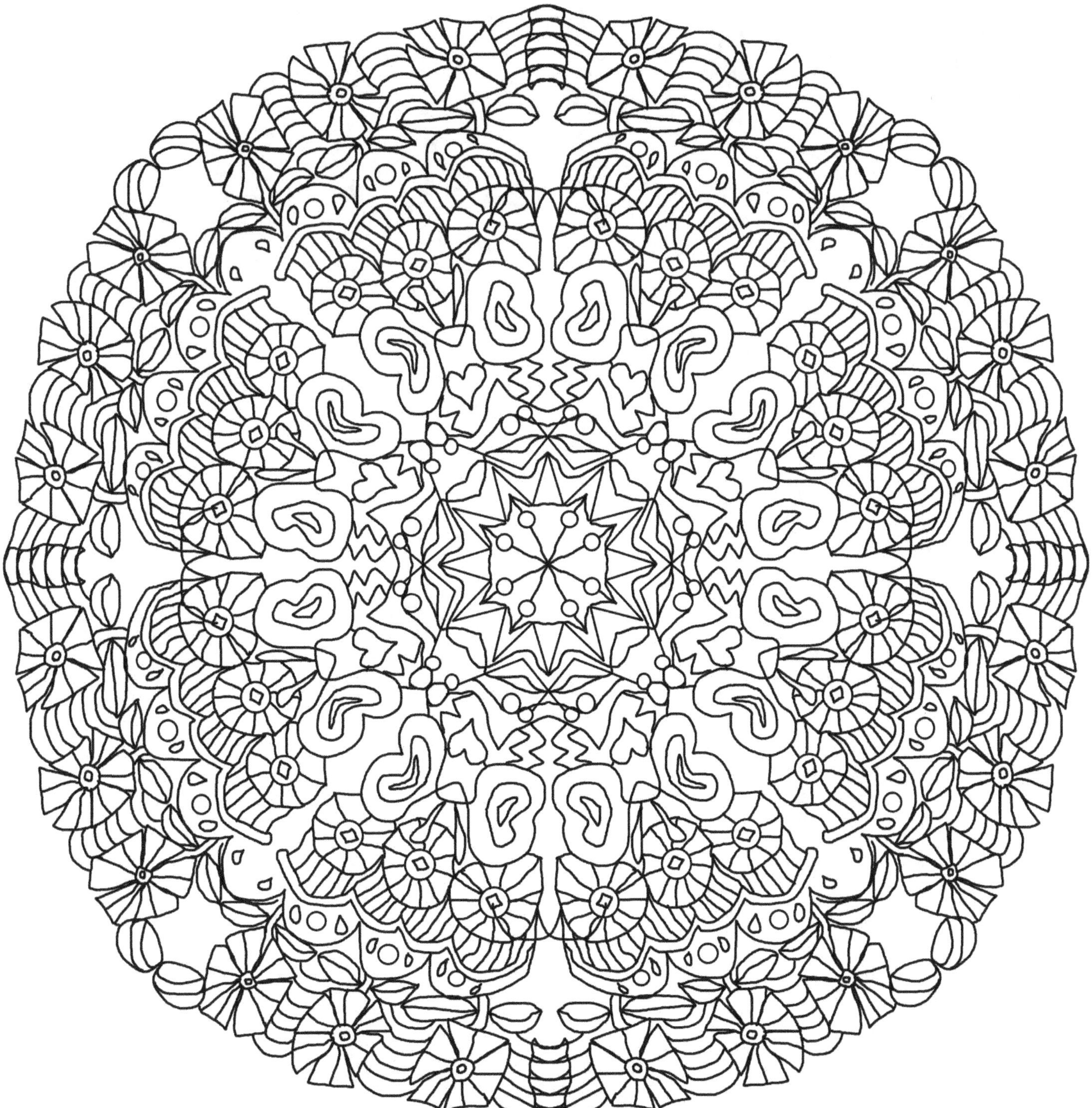

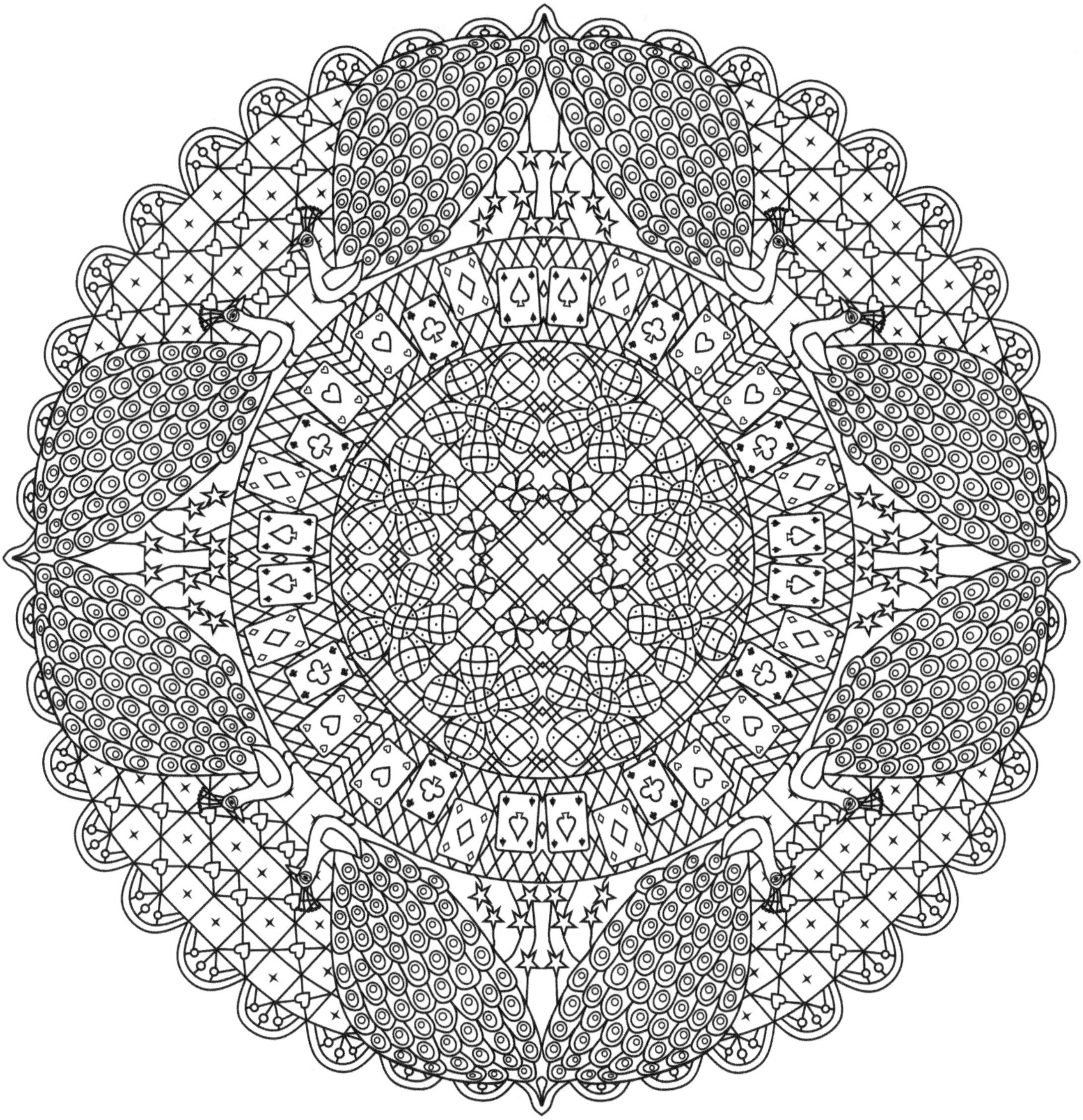

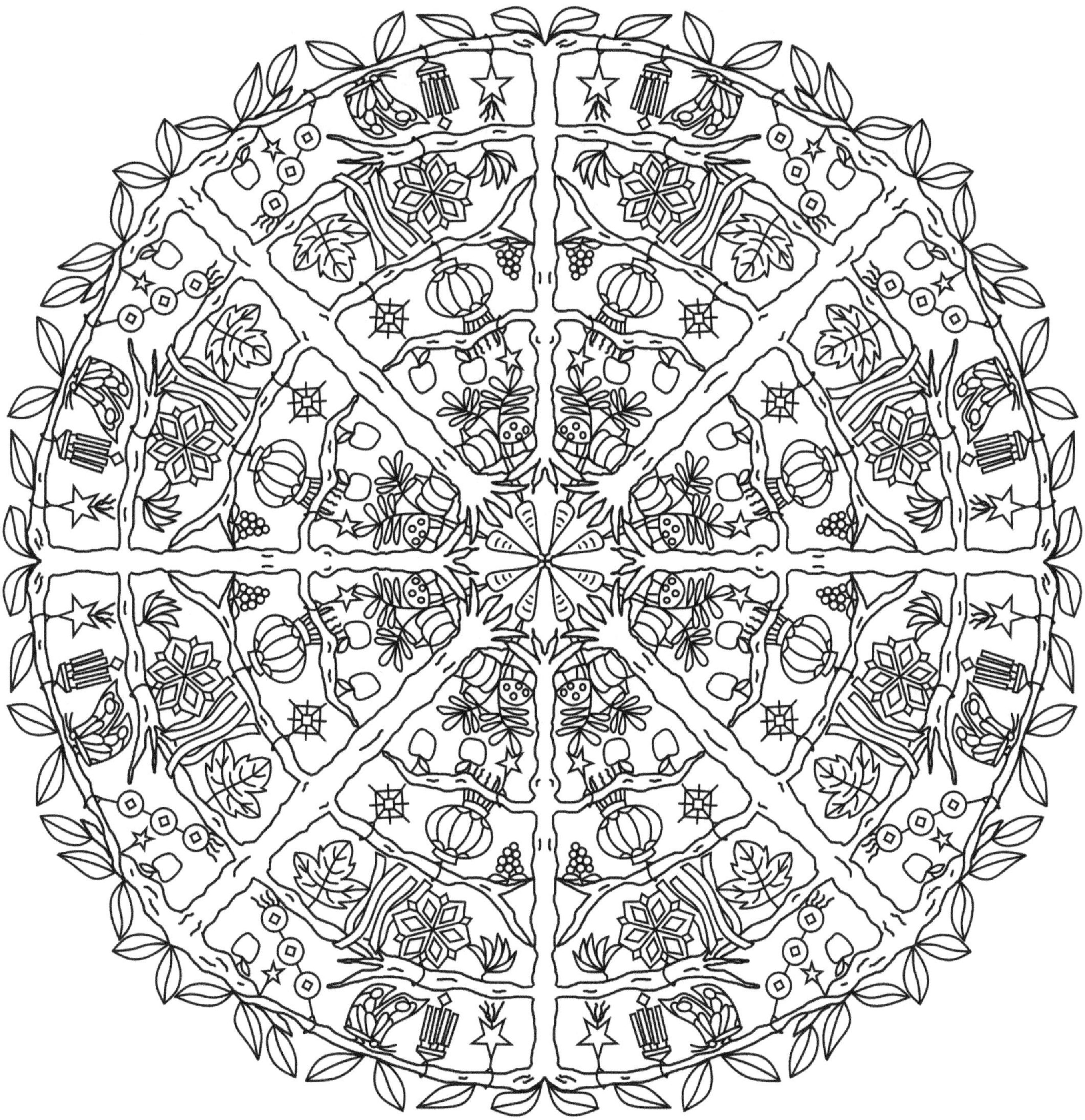

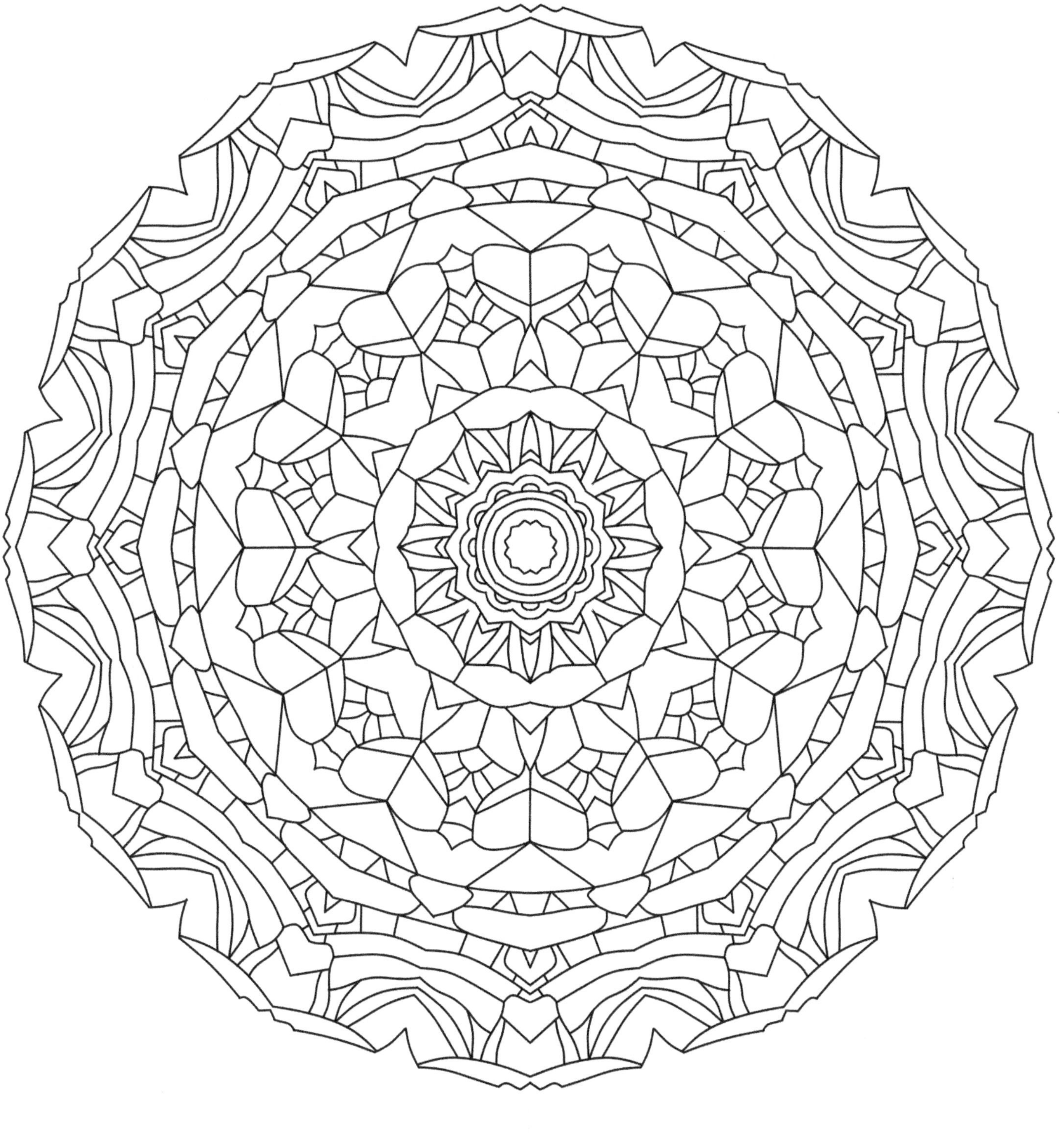

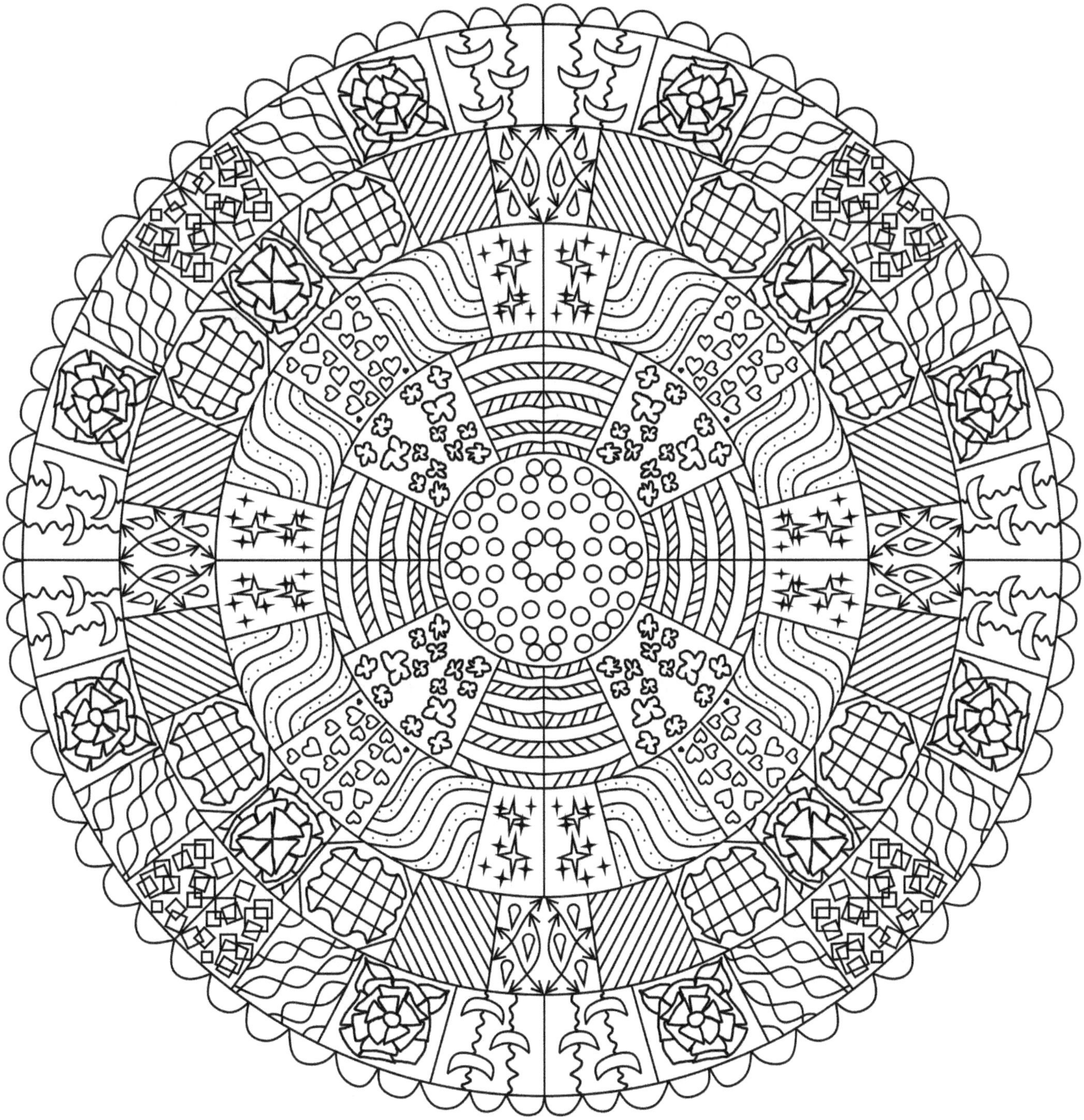

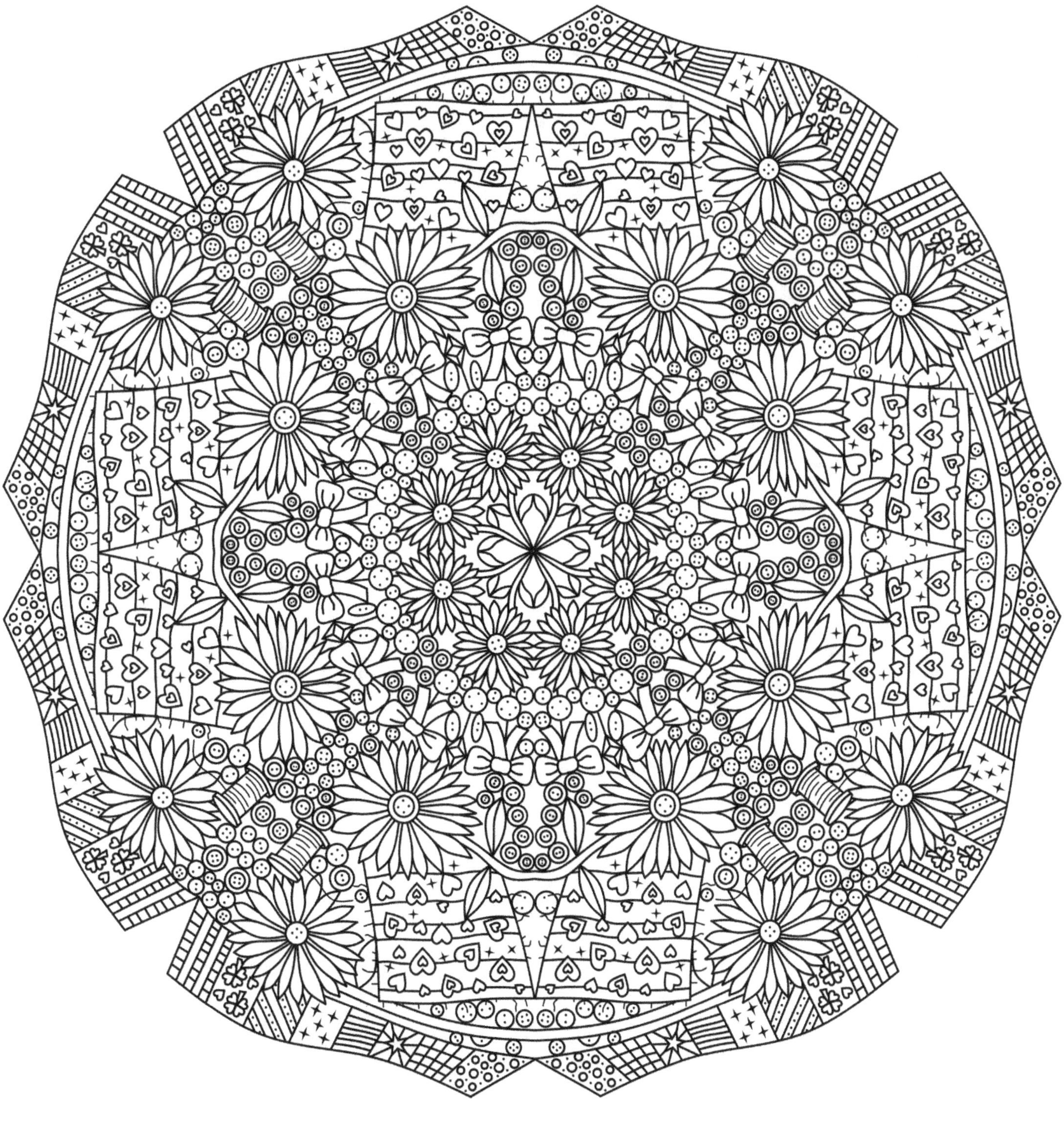

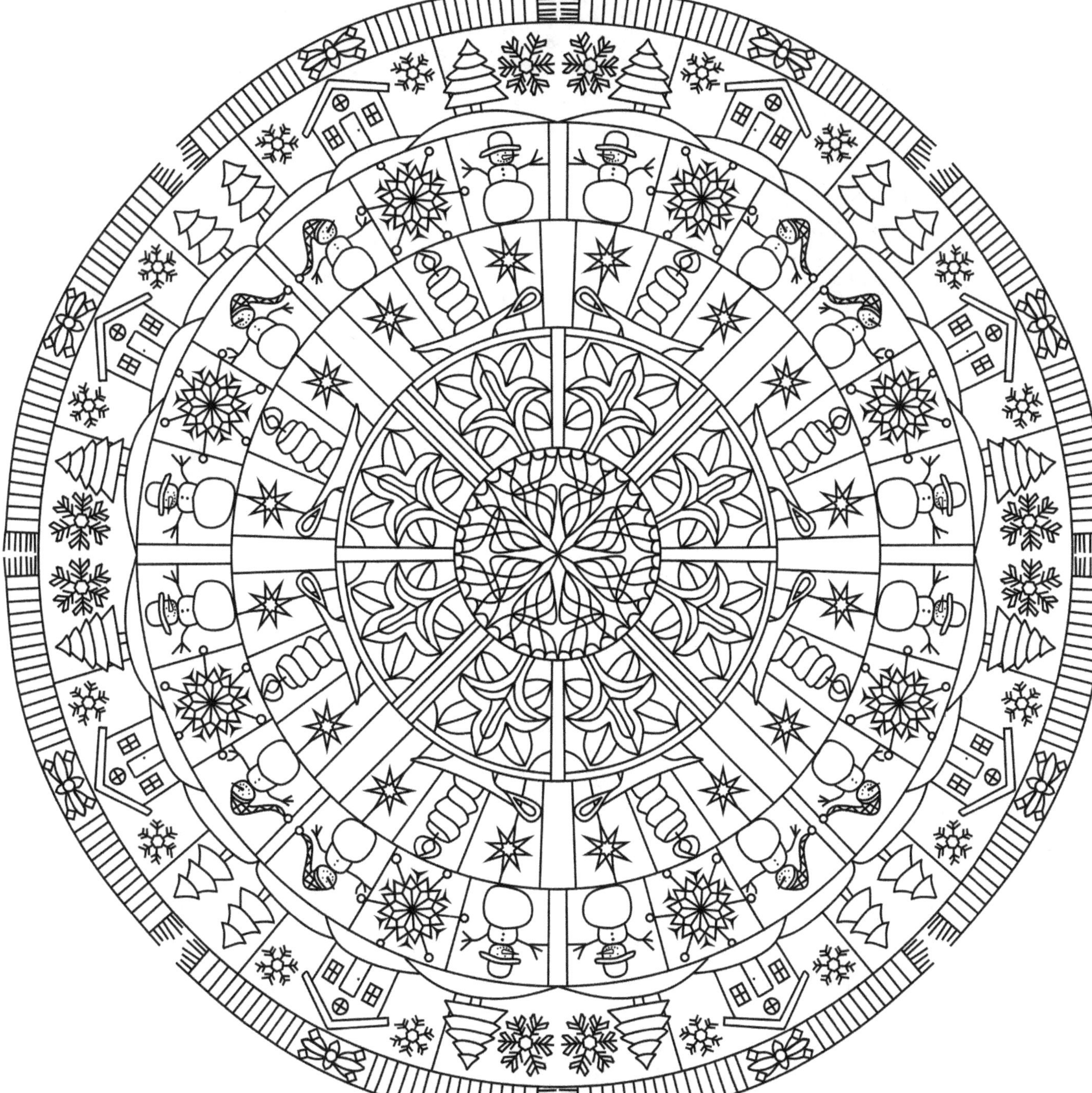

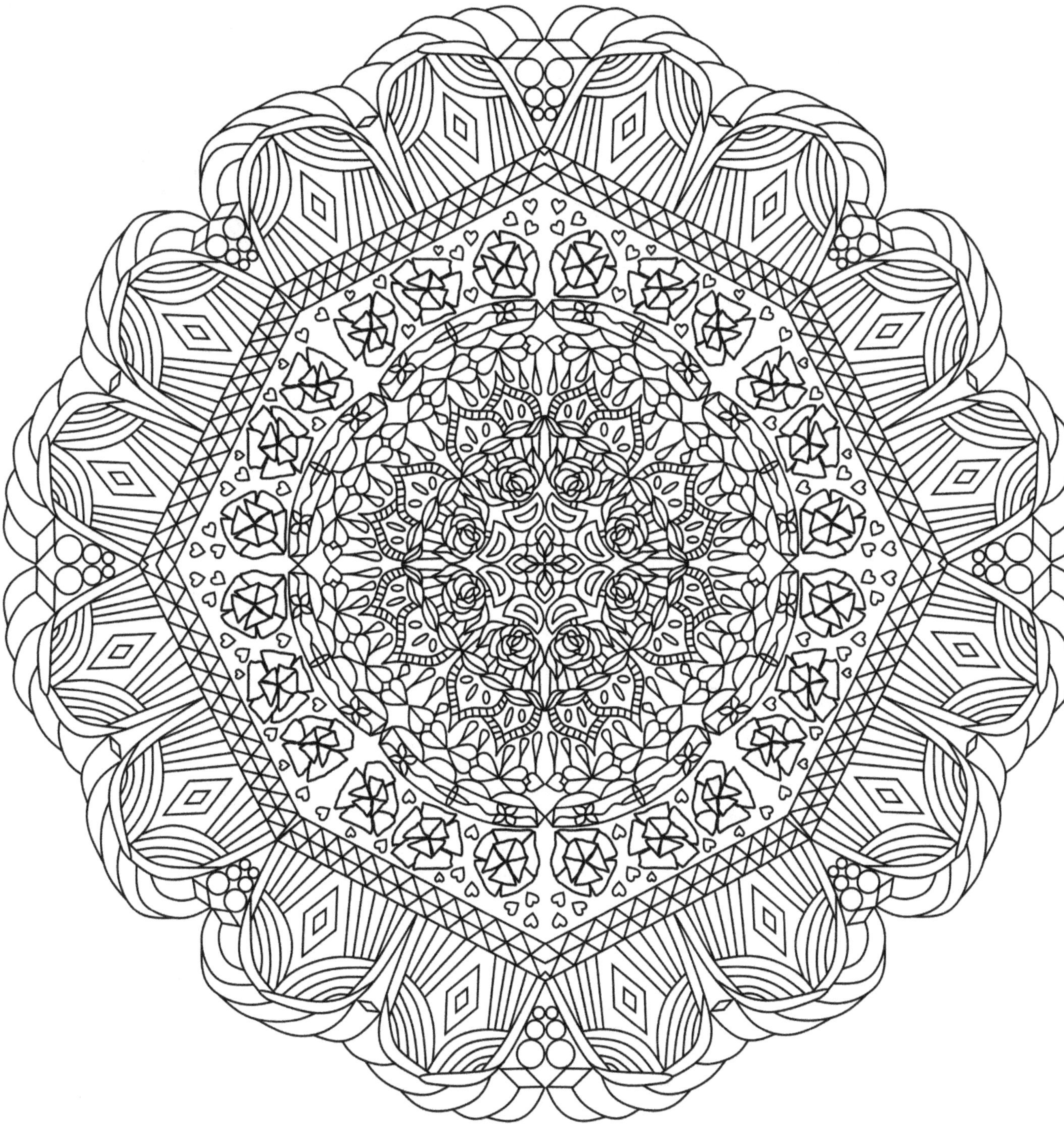

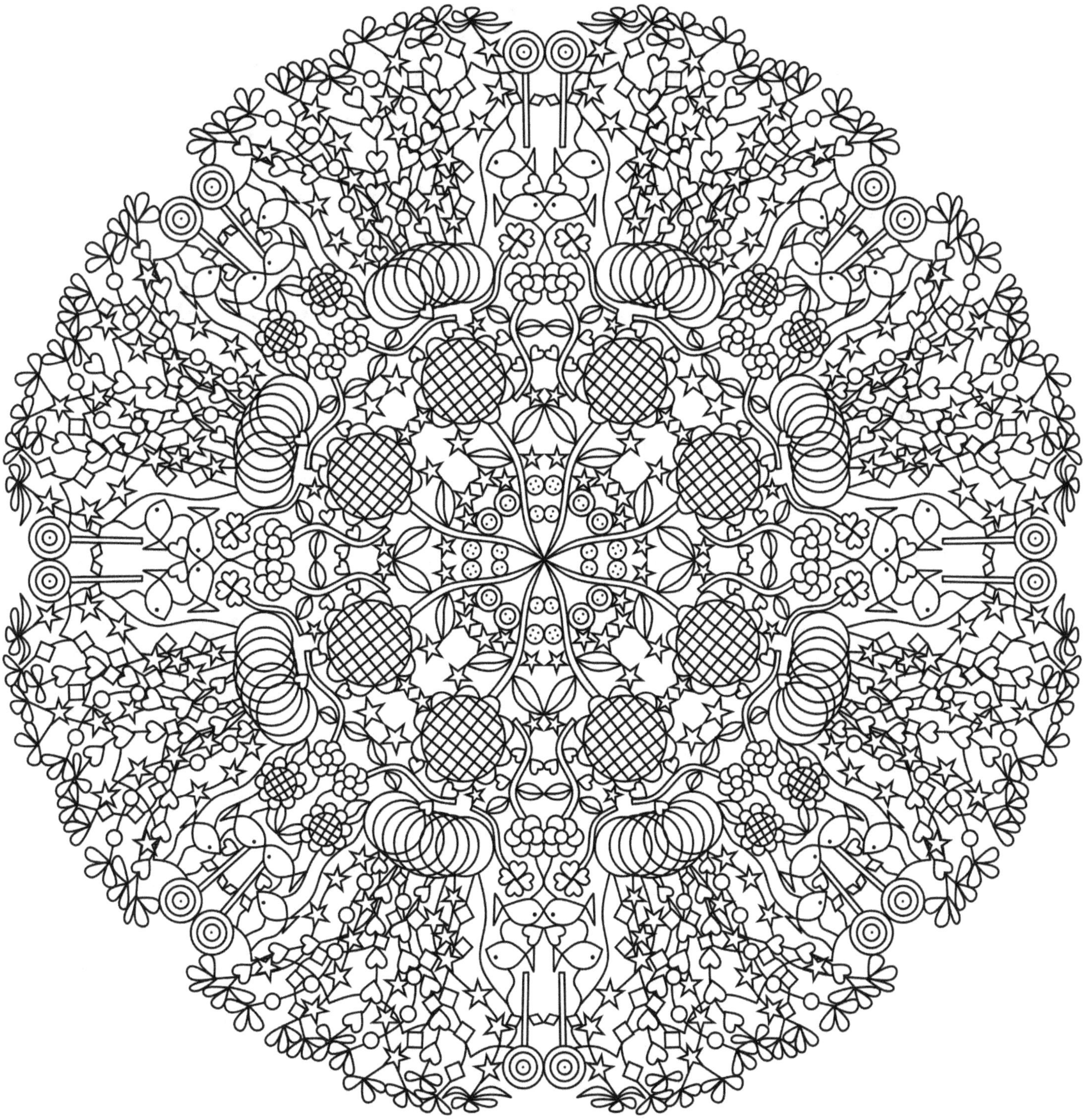

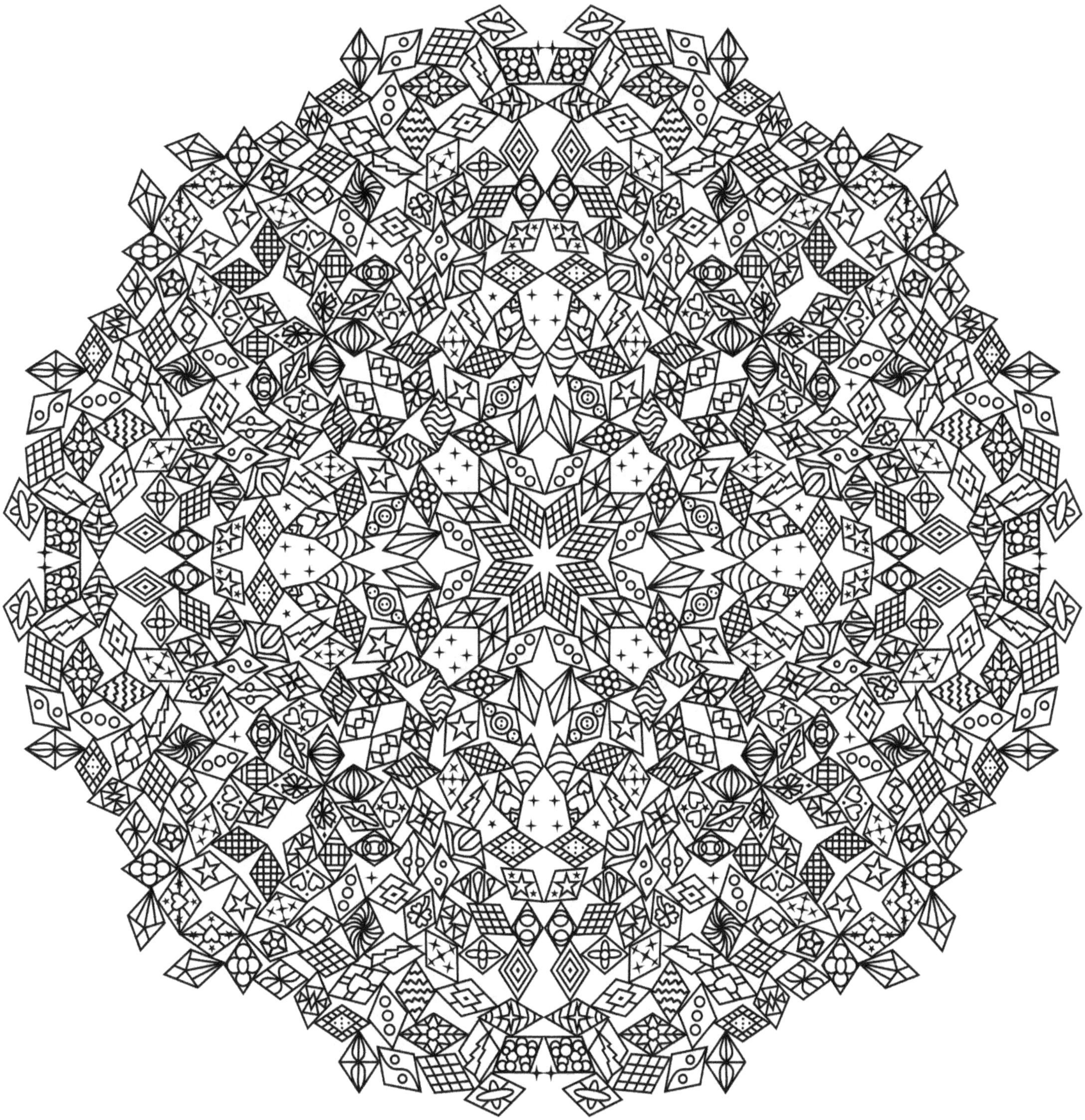

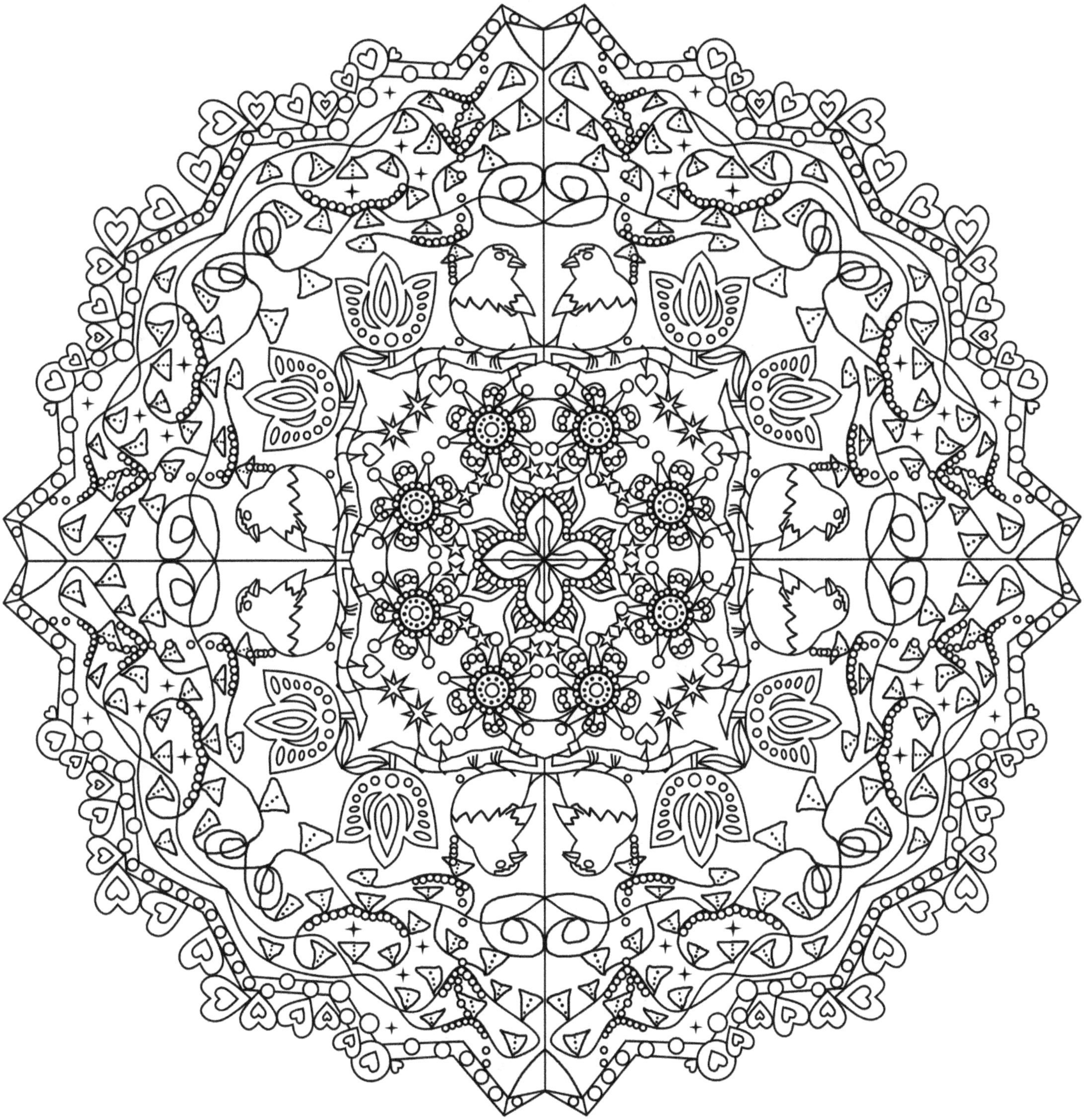

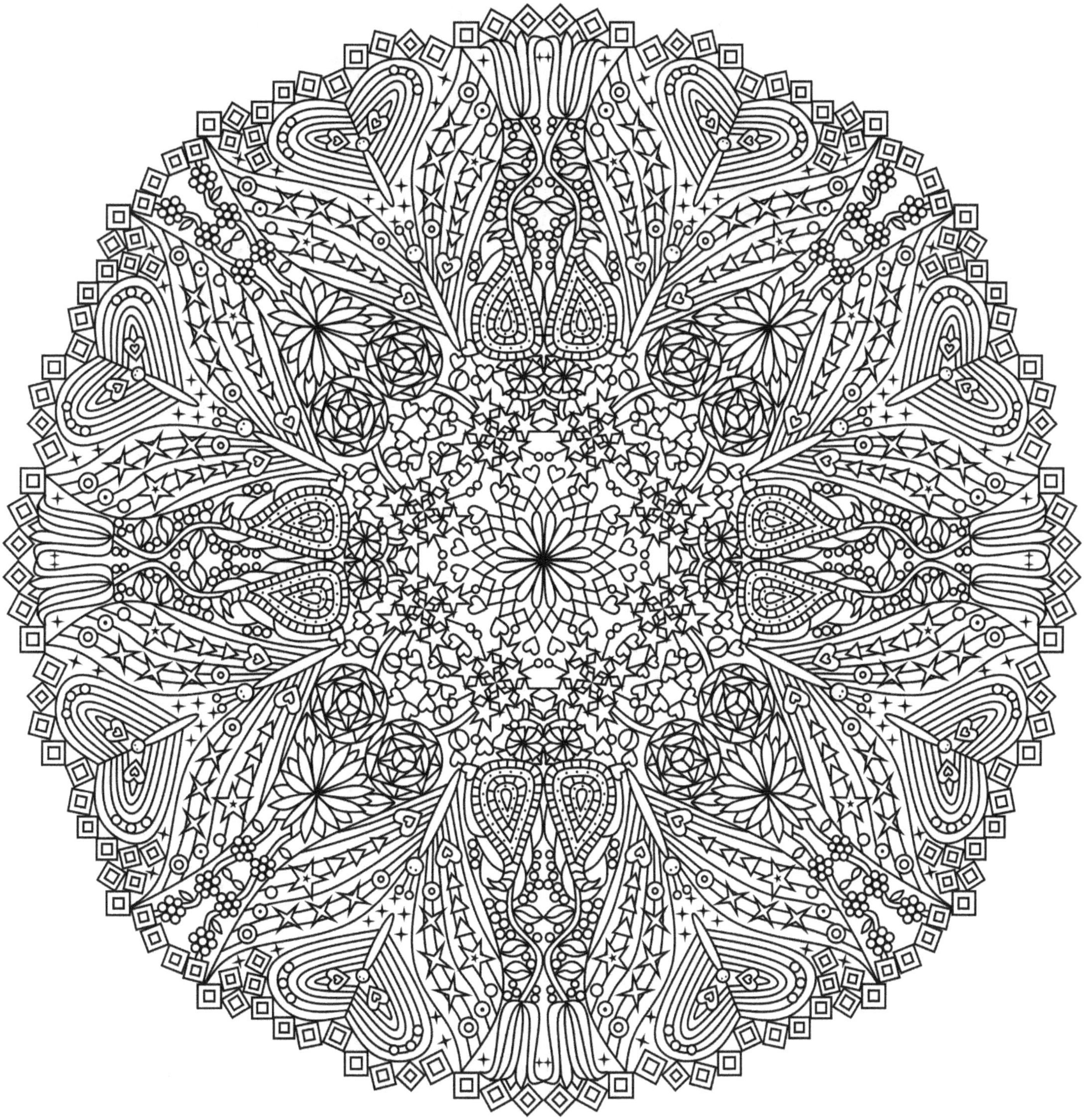

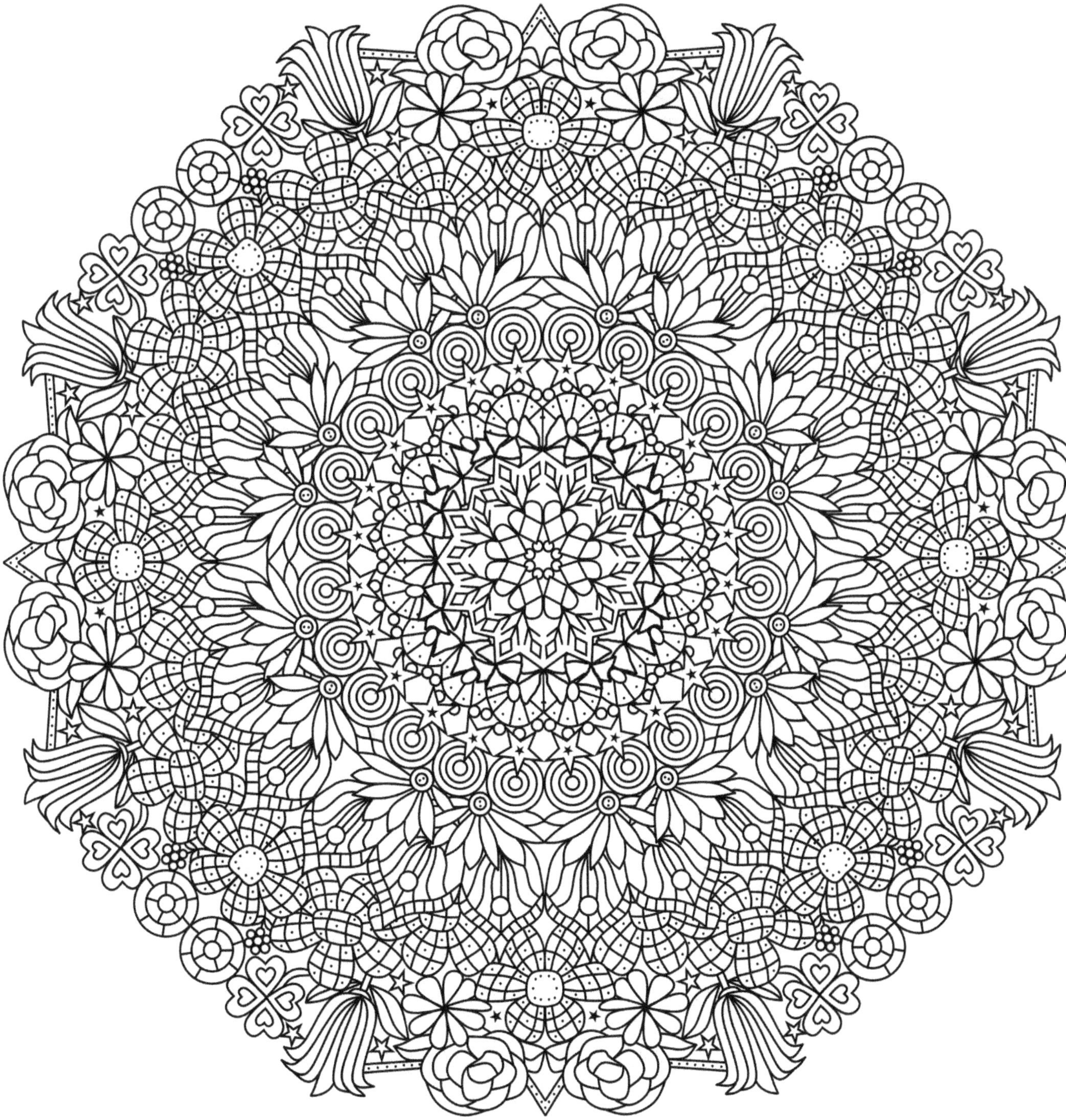

www.ingramcontent.com/pod-product-compliance
Lightning Source LLC
Chambersburg PA
CBHW080835180526
45168CB00006B/2696